T0090877

Total Tripping

USA

CARL LAHSER

Order this book online at www.trafford.com
or email orders@trafford.com

Most Trafford titles are also available at major online book retailers.

© Copyright 2014 Carl Lahser.
All rights reserved. No part of this publication may be reproduced, stored in a retrieval
system, or transmitted, in any form or by any means, electronic, mechanical, photocopying,
recording, or otherwise, without the written prior permission of the author.

Printed in the United States of America.

ISBN: 978-1-4907-4601-2 (sc)
ISBN: 978-1-4907-4602-9 (e)

Because of the dynamic nature of the Internet, any web addresses or links contained in
this book may have changed since publication and may no longer be valid. The views
expressed in this work are solely those of the author and do not necessarily reflect the
views of the publisher, and the publisher hereby disclaims any responsibility for them.

Any people depicted in stock imagery provided by Thinkstock are models,
and such images are being used for illustrative purposes only.
Certain stock imagery © Thinkstock.

Trafford rev. 09/10/2014

www.trafford.com
North America & international
toll-free: 1 888 232 4444 (USA & Canada)
fax: 812 355 4082

Contents

Over the past 50 years I have been to numerous big cities, small towns and driven a lot of back roads. Included in this collection are stories from a lot of places with my own peculiar observations. Long rides. Historic sites. Museums. Good food. Enjoy.

Carl

Galveston, TX

8-13 October 2005
Carl Lahser

Hurricane Rita almost ruined our short time-share vacation to Galveston. The wind and rain struck a glancing blow from the SE quadrant of the storm three weeks before we were supposed to arrive. My wife, Carol, called a couple days before we were scheduled to leave and was told everything was back on track.

We left the house in San Antonio about 0900 up TX 78 to Seguin. There we got on US Alt 90 through Gonzales, Shiner, Hallettsville, Eagle Lake, and Rosenberg. We took TX 36 to Lake Jackson and Freeport then the toll road to Galveston. We arrived at the condo about 1500 and checked in.

The toll road was not taking tolls. Like many other beach roads in the US there were houses between the highway and the beach. Several communities lined the road with houses built on stilts. A couple had siding or roofing missing from the hurricane. Many of the cabins looked like bird houses. The communities were interspersed with wetlands with some cattle and flocks of cattle egrets.

During the ride down there were occasional vultures and grackles. Most of the roadside vegetation was wind burned and yellow. We were in Lake Jackson before we saw any starlings, gulls, American egrets or pelicans. Along the beach were yucca, prickly pear, salt cedar thickets, and Spartina marshes.

I don't think the condo suffered storm damage – It was just run down. The condo was about 15 years old and looked like it had not been painted in years. Construction was wood frame and plaster instead of cement block. All of the windows were single hung glass that needed reglazing. These windows transmit street noise and lose heating and air conditioning. We found one cracked window pane which was promptly replaced using caulk instead of putty. The management was debating about charging us for the window. There were stains on the walls and ceiling indicating a leak. The "popcorn" ceiling treatment was flaking off and the AC outlets were rusted. Windows had Venetian blinds.

Cove molding, door casings and baseboards were of rough-sawn 1X2 lumber. Furniture looked like an "early marriage" mix of rattan, overstuffed chairs and sofa, French provincial, oriental, etc. The stair way was steep and the handrail was a 2X6 on one side. This would not pass an OSHA inspection

Downstairs consisted of a living/dining space with a kitchenette and half-bath and a deck. There were two small bedrooms with baths upstairs overlooking the street and beach. A common balcony connected the bedrooms upstairs. The GFI was not functional in one of the baths and nonexistent in the kitchen. Signs were posted on doors and windows to keep them shut because of humidity and sand.

I treat places like home and expect a facility at least as good a home since I was paying good money for the week. I was generally disappointed in the facility. If I wanted a cheap motel I would rent a cheap motel. I also did not like the clause that said if the hurricane had closed the place down we would lose our deposit and week. I should not have to pay for acts of God.

There were 20 units most of which were vacant. There was a small pool, a tennis court and basketball hoop, a small picnic area, and a small playground with a minimum of equipment.

The landscape pallet included oleander, ligustrum, and pittisporum with Bermuda grass. Invasive weeds included pennywort, bindweed, European daisy, frogbit, sandbur, Indian Blanket, dayflower, and dwarf dandelion.

About 1800 we went out for supper at Guido's. The restaurant had been on the beach for over a hundred years and I had not been there for over twenty years. Service and food were outstanding exceeding anything we saw in Italy several months previous. We began with an outstanding Sonora salad. Carol had center cut pork chops (4!) with baked tomatoes. I had baked redfish with crab meat. We took home some of the fish and two pork chops which I had for breakfast over the next two mornings.

Later we took a walk along the beach. The tide was out and the shells were a rubble of broken pieces on hard packed tan sand.

Sunday morning I was up before the sun and watched Casablanca. The sun finally came up through the scud which burned off into a bright clear blue sky.

I went for a walk on the beach watching the birds. Bonaparte's Gulls. One had a single leg. Willets. Sanderlings including one with a single leg. Brown Pelicans. Semipalmated Plovers. Cormorants.

After breakfast we crossed the street to the beach. There are stairs down the face of the seawall about every half mile. Groins of large granite cubes extend out about two hundred yards about every half mile to retard sand migration, reduce riptides, and provide fishing access. Signs say no swimming but the surfers paddle out near the end of the groins to catch waves. Looking back at the seawall we could see the fish murals decorating the concrete face.

From the bedroom balcony we could see one off-shore oil drilling platform and a steady stream of empty tankers heading for the loading docks in the Port of Houston or full tankers heading to refineries in Beaumont and other Texas ports. There were also trawlers working off the beach and an occasional workboat heading out to the off-shore oil rigs.

About 1000 we drove over to Moody Gardens. The Moody family was prominent in early Texas and Galveston development. The family decided to do something nice for the city and began developing a theme park about 15 years back. The grounds now contain a large hotel and conference center, a picnic grounds and sports fields, a riverboat and dock, a pyramid for an aquarium, another pyramid for science discovery exhibitions, and a third pyramid containing a tropical forest with butterflies and tropical birds. There is an IMAX theatre, several places to eat, and several gift shops. The grounds are landscaped with low maintenance plants. A ticket to see everything runs about $60.

As we entered the grounds there were birds in the drainage canals. Rosette spoonbills. Sanderlings. We visited the aquarium, the IMAX, and the tropical forest. The aquarium was well designed with theme tanks, interpretive signage and a large, well stocked central tank. The forest contained a variety of plants arranged by geographical areas. Birds, butterflies, and a pair of sloths roamed at will. The IMAX was a small IMAX theatre with a presentation on African wildlife. We left about 1630 and went back to the condo.

Monday morning a front was passing through. Clouds. Ten mph wind. The water was a gray-green. Higher waves. More birds on the beach. Later it began to rain.

About 1000 we went to the Strand and wandered one end to the other in the rain. The vendors had changed since we were in Galveston 15 years before. There were more T-shirt and tourist junk shops and less boutiques and good places to eat. Hendley Market and Bubba's military surplus were still there.

The same trend had occurred in New Orleans over the past 20 years. Night clubs became gay bars or female impersonator joints. Restaurants became custard shops and coffee bars. Jazz bars charging admission. The French Quarter and Hollywood looked neat at night but filthy in daylight. Galveston was relatively clean in daylight.

Lunch was at a neat little place that still had refrigeration problems. We returned to the condo about 1500.

Next morning we decided to hit art galleries. We set out looking for the Galveston Gallery and found it was a designer studio. The owner gave us a list of venues that turned out to have been the previous weekend. We drove around randomly looking at the old neighborhoods. There was little storm damage. After the seawall had been completed the island was backfilled and the homes were raised to get them above the 20 foot storm surge. They were not raised enough to use the space below most of the homes. Garages were too small to get modern cars into and many of them are not accessible from the street. Much of the town is under architectural control and zoning. Hundred year old houses cost about $200,000 plus $200,000 to bring them up to code and another $200,000 for antique furnishings.

We found the Galveston Art Center on the Strand. It had a show of aviation water colors and water colors of historical homes. They had a museum store selling local art.

We found a shop selling African art and antiques in the Strand Lofts. We bought two Maasai batiks and some 18th century Kissie "money". Further down the street we made reservations for a tour of historic Galveston for the next morning.

Lunch was at an Italian place on the Strand. Meat balls and penne pasta with a tomatoie acid sauce. After lunch we went to see the movie about the 1900 Galveston storm and the life of Jean Lafitte.

According to the movie the hurricane that struck Galveston September 2-9, 1900, with a twenty-foot storm surge demolished much of the community and killed 6,000 – 10,000 people. It was filmed by Edison and visited by Clara Barton of the Red Cross. (There is another 2-hour film called "Isaac's Storm" on the history channel.) One with the results of the storm was construction of a 10 mile seawall 20 feet high and backfilled to raise the island. Web sites on the storm give a more complete picture. Total deaths before the storm died may have been 12,000. The storm began in the mid-Atlantic on 27 August. It hit the Leeward Islands and had passed Puerto Rico by 31 August. It hit Hispaniola and Jamaica. Then it crossed Cuba with 24 inches of rain in 48 hours of September 3 & 4. On September 5 it hit Key West. Although most storms crossed Florida and into the Atlantic this one hit a high pressure front and turned west. Out over the Gulf it was measured at 28.75mb and winds of 100 mph (Cat 4 storm). Besides the damage to Galveston many other towns were damaged. Texas City. Dickinson. Lamarque. Hitchcock. Arcadia. Alvin. Manvel. Brazoria. Columbia, Wharton. Houston. All sustained damage and maybe 2, 000 deaths, The storm turned north on a 200 mile wide track over Hempstead, Brenham and Temple into Oklahoma, Kansas, and Iowa. Minnesota had 5 inches of rain. Six loggers were killed in Wisconsin. It crossed Michigan and southern Lake Huron and hit Toronto with 50 mph winds on the 11th. Two ships were sunk in Lake Erie and there was a million bucks damage to agriculture. In the Maritime Provinces of Canada there was damage in Nova Scotia and Prince Edwards Island. The flood tide in the Bay of Fundy caused damage in New Brunswick. It crossed Newfoundland from Corner Brook to Gander and sunk much of the San Pierre fishing fleet. The storm crossed the north Atlantic to Scandinavia, across Russia and blew out in Siberia.

The fifteen minute story of Jean Lafitte was told from the viewpoint of a cabin boy on the brig USS Enterprise. Lafitte may have been born about 1780 in France or Hispaniola. He may have died in a hurricane in Yucatan in 1826 or possibly in St Louis in the 1840's.

Lafitte was a pirate and established the "kingdom" of Barataria in the swamps near New Orleans after 1803. He may have had a thousand men when he joined Andrew Jackson in saving New Orleans during the War of 1812.

Several years later he and his men were run out of town on 8 pirate ships. He settled on Galveston Island which he called the "Kingdom of Campeche" in 1817. Lafitte bought or otherwise acquired a mansion from the French pirate Louis-Michel Aury which Lafitte renamed "Maison Rouge". The upper level of the house was fortified and held canons that controlled the harbor. Warehouses and housing for his men were built.

A bad hurricane hit in 1818 and flattened the community and sunk the fleet. Some of the fleet was rebuilt and Lafitte continued to harass the Spaniards.

In 1820 President Madison declared war on pirates. The USS Enterprise anchored off Galveston. Lafitte was given until May 1821. Lafitte burned the town and left with his men during the night. Lafitte may have gone to Charleston or joined Bolivar in South America, or joined the pirates in Santo Domingo, or died of plague in Mexico.

We walked along the harbor passing Joe's Crabs, Landry's, Willy G's, Fishermen's Wharf and the cruise terminal where Carnival, Royal Caribbean and Princess Lines all docked. Back to the car. We drove north along Harborside Drive to Ferry Road near the north end of the island. We passed Apffel Park and Stewart Beach then drove south along the seawall to the condo. Neptune's Kingdom. Fantasy Island. Saltgrass. Mariner Inn. Hotel Galvez. Mermaid Pier. Murdock's Bathhouse. Ocean Grill. Flagship Hotel.

We are not night people. We went for a walk on the beach and crashed.

Wednesday morning I took a walk on the beach. The sunrise was pretty and the water was clearing up. Several surfers were out looking for waves.

About 0900 we drove to the Strand and parked. We were a half hour early for our tour so revisited a couple of shops while we waited. One of the women recommended a shop where Carol might find turn of the century clothing. She made clothes for the Dickens festival.

We and two ladies from Seattle boarded a van and were shown historic structures in the Strand District, the Lost Bayou Historic District, and the Silk Stocking National Historic District. Our guide had retired out of the tourist bureau. We also toured the historic Ashton home.

Ashton Home

When we returned we went to look at the Peanut Butter Factory antiques. This was a mall but had nothing of particular interest.

The seamstress we were to visit had hats and dresses both antique and copies. Carol picked out a hat and gloves to go with her 1908 dress for Heritage Day in San Antonio.

We decided to head home on Thursday instead of Friday. We were up early and packed up. Breakfast was at the Mariner Inn on the seawall. We cleaned up our condo and checked out about 1000.

Plants

Bermudagrass	Cynodon dactylon
Bindweed	Convolvus arvensis
Dayflower	Commelina diffusa
Dwarf Dandelion	Krigia occidentalis
European daisy	
Frogbit	Phyla incisa
Indian Blanket	Gallardia estavellas
Marsh Pennywort	Hydrocotyle umbellata
Oleander	Nerium oleander
Pittisporum	
Prickly Pear	Opuntia lindheimeri
Salt Cedar	Tamarix sp.
Sandburr	Cenchrus sp
Waxleaf Ligustrum	Ligustrum quihoui
Yucca	Yucca constricta

Birds

Pelicanidae
Brown pelican   Pelecanus occidentalis
Phalacrocoracidae
Cormorant   Phalacrocorax auritus
Ardedae
Cattle Egret   Bubulcus ibis
Great Egret   Aedea alba
Threskiornithidae
Rosette spoonbill   Ajaia ajaja
Carthartidae
Black Vulture   Coragyps atratus
Charadriidae
Semipalmated Plover   Charadrius semipalmatus
Scolopacidae
Willet   Catoptrophorus semipalmatus
Sanderling   Calidris alba
Larinae
Bonaparte's Gull   Larus philadelphia
Sturnidae
Starling   Sturnus vulgaris
Icteridae
Common Grackle   Quiscalus quiscula

OCTOBER 2006 WAS A BUSY MONTH

Minneapolis and Washington D.C.

October was a busy month with a trip to Minneapolis and another trip to the McGaheysville in the Shenandoah Valley of Virginia. I seldom had two TDY's in any single month before I retired.

Trip 1.

An old friend of ours, Pat Marlowe, spends summers' in Minneapolis and the rest of the year in San Antonio. She broke her leg and had a plate installed last June after driving up to Minneapolis and spent the summer in a rehab facility. She called to ask if I might be interested in driving her, her car and her cat from Minneapolis to San Antonio for expenses. Since I had nothing particular planned my wife said to charge on.

I flew to Minneapolis on Monday, 9 October. On Tuesday we closed up her house and loaded the car to leave Wednesday morning. It was cool in Minneapolis with highs in the forties. This was a big change from San Antonio's 70's. There had been snow and cold in Minneapolis the previous week so the leaves were past prime colors and falling off the trees.

Wednesday morning was overcast with light rain. Shortly after we pulled out it began to spit snow. Pat navigated us through town to Interstate 35. From there it was I-35 VFR direct to San Antonio about 1250 miles. The wet sloppy snowflakes continued across the Iowa border where the snow turned to cold rain. I have now seen my snow for the year.

Across southern Minnesota two Red-tailed Hawks (<u>Buteo jamaicensis</u>) were seen hunched up in bare trees along the highway. I guess they were waiting to head south. Several other Red-tails were seen in Iowa along with a Northern Harrier (<u>Circus</u> <u>cyaneus</u>). The white tail marking of a Rough-legged Hawk (<u>Buteo</u> <u>lagopus</u>) disappeared into a grove of trees. Several large flocks of small birds were sitting on electrical transmission tower cross bars. Road kills included a fox, several raccoons, and a skunk. Most of the corn and soybeans had been harvested and a few fields were planted with winter wheat.

Late afternoon saw us across the Missouri border. There were a lot more trees with some having gone through leaf drop or beginning to color up. There were a few more Red-tailed Hawks in Missouri. A medium size flock of Red-winged Blackbirds (Agelaius phoeniceus) was swooping and looping generally towards the SE. About sundown we stopped in Liberty, Mo., just outside Kansas City at Pat's regular motel stop on her round trips. Pat got a handicapped room for her and her cat. Since the motel was almost empty, they assigned me the handicapped room next door.

We departed about 0900 Thursday morning to pass through Kansas City after the rush hour and head south. The rain had stopped and traffic flowed smoothly in spite of a lot of construction.

We went down I-35 to Emporia and got on the Kansas turnpike to the Oklahoma border. The turnpike was rather dull - rolling pastured hills with nothing but scattered cattle in sight, a few silos visible in the distance, and a train track and freight train way to the west. Driving 65 mph in moderate traffic with a lot of trucks on your tail does not leave much time for sightseeing.

Oklahoma was more hills but with a lot more trees. Streambeds and country road were marked by rows of trees. The highway crossed several rivers and there were signs pointing the way to wildlife reserves and recreational lakes. A few Western Meadowlarks (Sturnella neglecta) made short low flights from the roadside to open fields. We passed Oklahoma City in early afternoon and crossed the Texas border, as the sun was getting low.

Pat's next regular stop was a motel in Gainesville, Texas. Great-tailed Grackles (Quiscalus mexicanus) were invading the trees on their way south.

Next morning we were on the road about 0900 and took I-35W through Fort Worth and were in San Antonio about 1400. I unloaded the car at Pats and my wife came to pick me up. It was good to be back in the warm Texas sun.

Trip 2.

We had finally disposed of our time-shares although we had to pay a company to take them. We still had a week left on the books and Carol wanted to go to see Washington, DC. The closest and only timeshare near DC was Massanutten Resort located near McGaheysville in the Shenandoah Valley of Virginia. This happened to be 130 miles from downtown DC near Harrisonburg and the Skyline Drive/Shenandoah National Park near numerous Civil War battlefields and the heart of Stonewall Jackson's early campaigns.

Lots of nature watching was promised. Turning fall leaves. Hiking. Birding. The trees leaf color had peaked about a week before. Birds were essentially gone except for resident Mockingbirds (<u>Mimus</u> <u>polyglottus</u>), Mourning Doves (<u>Zenaida</u> <u>macroura</u>), and a few American Crows (<u>Corvus</u> <u>branchyrhyncos</u>). Several kettles of Turkey Vultures (<u>Cathartes</u> <u>aura</u>) were forming up over the ridges to fly to Panama for the winter. There were hiking trails but they were closed for hunting season.

Our flight from San Antonio to DFW was on time but the connecting flight was weather delayed and then held up almost two hours waiting on a parts. From the air the hills of Tennessee and Virginia were rusty red with fall color.

Virginia Red Hills from the Air

Washington subdivisions were scattered in the trees with numerous white roofs looking like a kicked over termite colony. We arrived at Dulles two hours late. Flying certainly has changed since I began riding the friendly skies forty years back. The current two-hour early check-in is a nuisance. Paperless tickets are no great saving if you need to check a bag. I am happy the flights are all no smoking now but most airlines have also eliminated meals (But they sell box lunches.) Long time ago, if a plane was delayed, the bar was opened but now everyone flies dry and second-class. I'm waiting for passengers having to strip and put on an orange jumpsuit and check ALL baggage with no carry-on.

First time I flew into Dulles was in the late 1970's. There was one terminal building sitting in the middle of a maze of runways in undeveloped country NW of Fairfax, Virginia. They used big funny looking doublewide busses, called mobile lounges that drove out to the planes to load/unload passengers. I about panicked that first time when I saw the time between flights was three minutes instead of the usual couple hours. No problem. You got off one lounge and walked a few feet to get on the next lounge out to your new plane.

We drove out of Dulles on US 28 to I-66 heading west. Considering encroachment and continued construction we got lost a couple times but we were on the right road by 1500. Most of the leaves were gone except some that had been caught in a freeze and still hanging on. On one stretch of highway lavender Cosmos was still in bloom. Traffic was smooth at steady 65 mph with beaucou trucks. All the little towns were off the road.

We finally passed through Front Royal, as the sun was hitting the horizon and turned south on I-81. The sun was gone by the time we arrived at Harrisonburg. We turned on US 33 trying to follow the detailed written instructions we had been given. I finally stopped at a gas station for directions and got directions that were much less confusing, "Stay on this road about ten miles until you see a new Exxon station and turn left." We found US 33 was called something different through each little town such as the Jackson Highway.

It was dark by the time we checked in and it took a couple passes to find the right unlighted street to our condo.

Monday morning we had a tour of the facility. 6000 acres. 1500 condo units plus a hotel and ski lodge. Three golf courses. Indoor and outdoor water parks. Stables. A zillion colorful trees. Just what some people like for an annual vacation. About 0900 I remarked on two kettles of vultures forming up along the ridgeline to migrate to Mexico. One of the guests said it was probably something dead attracting the birds.

We were supposed to be in a new luxury condo. Here are a few observations based on reviewing plans and specifications in the military and private fields over the past 40+ years. You enter into a living/dining room. There were two utility closets in this room. The fireplace had no hearth, which violates fire codes most places. The kitchen intruded into the living room. If the bathroom doors are open the toilet was visible from the living room sofa and dining table and from the stove in the kitchen. Furnishings were commercial grade and commercial grade carpet and vinyl flooring were used. The floor sheeting must be 3/8 inch since it bounced. The bathroom was oversize like exercise equipment or a washer and dryer were supposed to be there. The bedroom was large and had a hot tub in the corner, which reminded me of sleeping in the bathroom. View from the porch was of the parking lot and dumpster. I'm afraid my idea of luxury is different from that of the management. It was utilitarian and better than some timeshares we had used but not luxury.

We spent Monday afternoon shopping for groceries and finally found a Food Lyon in a shopping center and a store called "A Million Books". We also stopped at two antique shops that had much the same as our local San Antonio shops.

On Tuesday we drove south on back roads to I-64 and Waynesboro. Just east of town was the entrance to Skyline Drive and Shenandoah National Park. We looked for the visitor center the sign indicated. The entrance leads to a battered, long closed Howard Johnsons diner and a closed motel. Around the corner and down the hill was another old building with a visitor center sign. Guess the Park Service was short money or the local Congressmen don't have any pull. Entering the park road there was a sign to pay when you left the park. The park road is about 100 miles long from Rockfish to Front Royal. The road was well maintained with numerous overlooks and campgrounds and would make a wonderful Sunday afternoon drive.

There had already been freezes and high wind so the color of the leaves was past prime. There was mist that looked like smoke in some of the valleys. Some of these gray areas were snags in previously burned areas that had not yet revegetated. Gray snags were visible mixed with young broadleaf regrowth. Interpretive signs explained watersheds, forest fires, and the historical highlights of the Shenandoah Valley. Visitor centers and campgrounds were closed for the season.

Shenandoah Valley

Sky Line Drive

The only plants in bloom were the white (<u>Aster</u> <u>ericoides</u>?) and blue asters (<u>Aster</u> <u>simplex</u>) along the park road. Milkweed (<u>Asclepias</u> <u>quadrifolia</u> and <u>A.</u> <u>tuberose</u>) pods were open and the silky parachutes were mostly gone. Smooth sumac (<u>Rhus</u> <u>glabra</u>) and Staghorn Sumac (<u>Rhus</u> <u>typhina</u>) leaves were adding color to the roadside vegetation. Witch-hazel (<u>Hamamelis</u> <u>virginiana</u>) had bloomed out. Several gray and green shale outcroppings had lichens. Moist seeps had ferns, mosses, and liverworts. Trees included several species of pines, oaks, elms, and maples.

We turned off at Swift Run Gap as the sun was nearing the horizon. The exit had a sign saying to drive on through so we did.

Wednesday we had a bus trip to see the sights of Washington, DC. Washington is not my favorite city but Carol had lived in DC twice and I had visited it many times. Neither of us had been there in several years. I figured that a two hour bus ride beat driving and parking.

First stop was the Marine Corps War Memorial or Iwo Jima statue of raising the US flag on Mount Suribachi. This was the first time I had ever walked around it or watched the Marines march by.

Iwo Jima Monument

Second stop was Arlington National Cemetery with the Tomb of the Unknown Soldier, the Kennedy Memorial, the new Woman's Memorial, and thousands of graves. We had both seen much of the cemetery over the past forty years so we spent our time at the Woman's Memorial. Carol found her name and picture in the registry.

Arlington Headstone

Sgt D. C. JONES
1921-1944
on the reverse
SARA JONES
BELOVED WIFE
1924-1996

Together again.

*****

We drove past the Pentagon and the impressive new Air Force Memorial and stopped at the Pentagon City Mall for lunch. The mall was much cleaner and better organized than I remembered. Then we drove past the Capitol.

Air Force Memorial near the Pentagon

I remember riding through downtown on the way to the airport early one morning.

Columbus Circle at 4 AM in July

Its sticky and cool.
Every bench sleeps at least
one homeless body.
Almost no traffic
but the signals work religiously.

+++++

We got off the bus near the Capitol, the Supreme Court, and the Library of Congress. The Court was closed so we entered the Library of Congress. This was my first time since 1962 when I brought some folk song tapes from Newfoundland. I checked the catalog and found one of my books listed. Three others were in the archives and two others were wherever they store the books sent for Library of Congress numbers.

We walked around the Capitol to the bus stop to wait for the bus. We rode along the Mall and passed the Washington Monument. I have walked the Mall along the reflecting pool several times watching the joggers, walkers, and tourists and the squirrels attacking the garbage cans. Traffic was rerouted around the White House and the area around the White House was blocked off with construction so that the White House was not even visible.

Next stop near the relatively new World War Memorial. This was impressive. We walked from there to the Vietnam Memorial wall with few visitors, which I had seen once before. The first time I visited the Memorial there were several protesting veterans camped nearby. The wall had uniforms, boots and medals left by friends and family of those named. Lots of people made rubbings of the names carved into the wall.

We saw the new Vietnam Women's Memorial and the new Korean War Memorial installed since I was last in DC in 2002. These were new impressive bronze statues. We are getting too many monuments or, maybe, too many wars.

World War Memorial

Vietnam Wall

Here is my old poem about the wall.

Black Horizon
The Vietnam Memorial

Cross the mall from the Smithsonian
to the T-shirt stand by the crosswalk
then up the hill to the Washington Monument
encircled with flags and hundreds of people waiting in line.

Down the hill to the Reflecting Pool
with a view of the Lincoln Memorial to the west
and the Capitol and the Washington Monument eastward.

A father was telling his young sons about the anti-war protest
when a million people filled the Mall
and one of the boys asks, "Like in Forest Gump?"

Tent with a hunger striker and Vietnam vets
lying in the grass protesting.

Up and over a berm a grove of trees appears.
Descending the berm the green of the grass surrenders
as under the canopy of the trees
a dark horizon dawns in the afternoon sun.
A black marble mass takes shape.

All those names and none were personal friends.
This is a monument to a young man's war.
Flowers and a service jacket with ribbons,
people touching names on the wall,
people making paper impressions of special names.
We all owe God a death and hope the death has value.

A long quiet walk back along the Reflecting Pool
As joggers and the resident squirrels scurry past.
Carl 950713

We walked on to the Lincoln Memorial, which had been cleaned in the past year. The view of the Washington Monument in the Reflecting Pool was still impressive after over forty years.

Next stop was the white-domed Jefferson Memorial. I had seen this numerous times flying in and out of Anacostia Naval Air Station that became Washington National Airport that was now Reagan Airport. This was the first time I had actually been in it.

The last stop was the new Roosevelt Memorial. The sun was setting and it was getting cool. This relatively new Memorial was very impressive with four water walls of increasing impressiveness representing the increasing importance of Roosevelt's terms. There were numerous bronze statues including Roosevelt seated in a wheelchair.

Roosevelt in his Wheelchair

It was a two-hour drive to Front Royal and supper. We arrived home about 2200.

Thursday we drove over to see Monticello and the Michie Tavern near Charlottesville, VA. Monticello is on the SE side of town on private foundation property. Jefferson was an impressive character and his house had a lot of unique innovations. We toured the house and grounds and walked through the woods to the family cemetery and on to the visitor's center.

We drove a couple miles to see Michie Tavern. This historic roadhouse and stage stop was originally located on the north side of Charlottesville. It had a decent lunch and an interpretive tour including a two-hole outhouse. We were back home by 1800.

Friday was highlighted by a visit to the New Market Battle Field. We drove north to the town of New Market and followed the signs to the New Market Battlefield State Historical Park. The Hall of Valor had interpretive displays. They showed a movie about the battle where the Virginia Military Institute Cadet Corps joined General Breckenridge in repulsing the Union attack in the Battle of the Field of Lost Shoes. We then walked the battlefield around the restored Bushong farm and the battlefield itself. On this cool clear day in November it was difficult to see a cool rainy May in 1864.

Field of Shoes

We drove through New Market and stopped for a late lunch of southern fried chicken. We were back home by dark.

Saturday morning we drove to the Artisans Center of Virginia at Waynesboro. This was a state subsidized outlet for local artists. There were some very good pieces of quilting, carving, carpentry, pottery, and painting.

On the way home we stopped at a county craft sale at the Shenandoah regional high school. This was primarily an outlet for a countywide crafts guild. Interesting but nothing we could not do without.

Sunday morning we checked out and drove back to Dulles. Trees were barer than the previous Sunday. The plane to Dallas was on time but we were on different planes to San Antonio. We were home by late afternoon.

New Orleans, LA

June 2013

This is the tale of a trip to New Orleans to attend the American Association of University Women national convention June 9-12, 2013.

I had been to New Orleans several times in the past with fish culture meetings at Tulane University and LSU, and stops at Breaux Bridge to visit crayfish farms. We had also spent a timeshare week in New Orleans in 1985 mostly in the French Quarter.

Carol and I had scheduled a Caribbean cruise out of New Orleans in December of 2012. Carol's back acted up and required treatment so we cancelled the cruise. We had decided to ride Greyhound from San Antonio to New Orleans partially because of price and partially because the cruise ship dock was near the bus station. Greyhound refused to refund the ticket price for any reason but graciously allowed that if we paid another $40 they would reissue the tickets for use anytime within a year. We rebooked Greyhound for the following June to attend a conference in New Orleans.

We boarded the bus on Saturday evening, 8 June, and spent the night freezing and sitting on what in Mexico would be classed as a second class bus with the seats and floor vibrating like a WWII cargo plane. The bus arrived in New Orleans about 0700 Sunday morning. Our bags arrived but Carol's walker did not. Greyhound said when they found it they would deliver it to our hotel.

A taxi delivered us to the Sheraton Hotel on Canal St. a little past 0800. We were pleasantly surprised to find they had a room ready for us on the 35th floor. After moving in we went to breakfast and arranged for an afternoon tour of New Orleans.

Canal St from our room to NW. Lake Pontchartrain on the horizon. Red buildings right of center is Storyville (the old red light district named after Mayor Story). Storm clouds building.

New Orleans at Night. Canal Street

The tour covered the French Quarter, the Garden District, Central Business District, Industrial District, the Ninth Ward and a stop by Cemetery No. 1. Everything but the Ninth Ward had pretty well recovered from the Hurricane Katrina flood. The French Quarter had had no flooding at all. The other areas had up to six feet of water. The Ninth Ward was covered by almost 20 feet when the levee was breached drowning a number of people. Homestead for Humanity built about 800 replacement homes, Opra built about 200 and Brad Pitt was still working on his 150 homes.

Garden District Home

The French Quarter looked pretty much like I remembered.

The Garden District houses were built high enough to escape major flood damage. Iron picket fences. Nine foot doors opening onto sixteen foot ceilinged rooms. Tall double and triple sash windows that served as doors when the bottom sash was opened. Mardi Gras beads still hanging in the trees and from the power lines not yet collected by the bead recyclers.

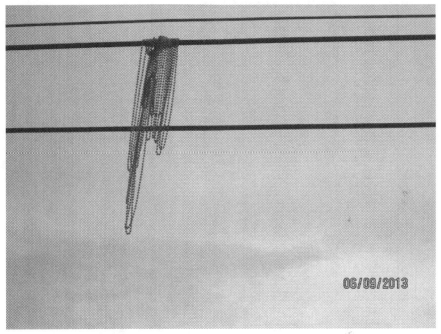

Mardi Gras Beads

About 255 million pounds of beads are shipped from China each year. About ten million pounds are used in NO for Mardi Gras each year. Lots of lead and heavy metals.

Many of the buildings in the Central Business District and the Industrial District were renovated or are being renovated incorporating an Arts District with museums and galleries. Friends that had lived in the Industrial District had to barricade themselves in the upper floors to avoid criminals and the homeless.

Some of the Ninth Ward still looked much like a war zone. Many of the small businesses and a few of the houses had been repaired and reopened. The major damage had occurred when a barge that had gotten loose wiped out the levee. As much as 20 feet of water rushed four blocks inland. Many of the residents of the Ninth ward did not own their homes and, with nothing to lose, have not returned after being bused who knows where.

The Brad Pitt houses were built on piles above the high water mark with solar power and access to the roof to prevent anyone being trapped inside in case of another flood. Still a lot of rebuilding needed.

The Katrina flood pointed out many flaws on the city's infrastructure like levees and flood gates that were over a hundred years old, no survival plans, and no recovery plans. City, state and federal agencies all failed. Then there were crooked officials and bigoted cops. Other cities should take notice but probably won't.

Final stop was at Cemetery Number One. This was one of several cemeteries in town. Since there is a high water table all burials are in vaults above ground. They are designed to hold a couple hundred bodies but not all at once. The body is removed a year and a day after burial, the bones crushed and then interred in a storage space under the vault.

Cemetery No. 1

We stopped for a break at the arboretum. Hot Chocolate and beignets with cinnamon sugar.

Carol checked in for the conference and attended a welcome dinner. I wandered off to the French quarter and had dinner at Galatoires. Galatoires is a 5-star restaurant and required a coat which they gladly loaned to me. I ordered etouffee and a sazerac for a nominal fee of almost $50. I thought about oysters but not for $20 a half dozen.

I passed The Famous Door and Pat O'Brian's with jazz you could hear half a block away. Might have been fun once but it's way too loud for me now.

Etouffee at Galatoires

Monday morning I went to Mena's Café for breakfast of grits and eggs then walked about eight blocks south on Magazine St to the WWII museum. Along the way I stopped at the Glassworks and Printmaking Studio to look at their glass work. Really good stuff.

The War in the Pacific Museum had expanded over the past few years. It is now the WWII Museum with three buildings covering almost a city block. Museum, theatre, aircraft and equipment. More was scheduled. Lots of dioramas and movie clips. The result of the efforts of hundreds of designers and historians. Manned by veterans. I recommend seeing this museum.

I stopped at Lee Circle and found the Civil War Museum was closed.

Lee Circle

Heading back to the hotel I stopped at the Contemporary Art Museum and the Ogden Museum of Southern Art. Both were open on Monday. Both had good exibitions.

Steve Martin art

I stopped at several galleriess and at the studio of Steve Martin. He did modern expressionism and wire sculpture.

Monday evening we went out for supper. We were leaving the hotel when the front desk said that Corol's walker had been delivered so we stopped to pick it up.

Since everyplace I suggested was beyond her walking distance we stopped at the Palace Café owned by one of the Brennan brothers of resturant fame. I had pecan fried catfish with a local Abati amber beer and bananas Foster for desert. Carol had a steak.

Tuesday morning I went to the Insectarium and then walked over half of the French Quarter. The Insectarium fronts on Canal St and belongs to a group of Audubon facilities in New Orleans. Exhibits were well done but primarily aimed at kids. There was a snack bar with an adjacent Bug Appetite that serverd bug dishes. Roasted meal worms with sugar and cinnimon or chili sauce and lime. Cricket cookies. Dips made with crisp meal worms in mayonaise and garlic. The gift shop specialized in insect related items.

Canal St Trolley

   I walked along Decatur St to the old Jax brewery. It is now a shopping mall with a couple of resturants. I continued on to the French Market and circled Jackson Square and passed St Louis Cathedral.

Jackson Sq

Along the south side of the square were shops and painters displaying art along the fence. Mule cars and taxicycles were lined up along Decatur St in front of the square. On a bench in front of the Cathedral sat several musicians with their instruments, taking a break. The Louisiana Art Museum was was closed for the day

Along St. Peter St were numerous shops and a few bars, including Pat O'Brians. I stopped for lunch at the Old Coffee Pot where I had last eaten 40 years ago. Grillins and grits.

I made a left on Royal St. and stopped at the court of Two Sisters to look. Hadn't changed a bit except the prices had doubled.

Pat O'Brians and Famous Door

It was hot and sunny so I jumped from one air conditioned antique shop or gallery to the next all along Royal Street to Canal.

Carol finished her meeting and was in the room when I got back. She got dressed and she went to the big hundred dollar a plate go home dinner.

I went out and about as the sun was disappearing for an oyster fix. The oyster bar had slurpies fixed half a dozen ways. Half a dozen and a beer ran $20. Used to buy a couple tow sacks full for that kind of money.

Oyster Bar

Wednesday morning we headed out for breakfast. I recommended Menas. She asked several people who also recommended Menas, so Menas it was. Grits and eggs for me and hot cakes for Carol.

It was about 0700. In the block's walk to the café, janitors were hosing off the building and sidewalk and the gutters flushing away the remnants of last night's carousing and homeless excrement. It's the price for a party town. At least they don't have parking meters to hang on to like San Francisco.

After breakfast, we walked over to Royal St and looked at antique shops and art galleries for a couple hours. Back at the hotel, someone recommended Lionels for lunch. Jambolaya with catfish for me and red beans and rice for Carol. That pretty well walks me through the menu of typical Cajun food.

Jambulaya and Catfish

We gathered up our stuff and headed to the bus station about 1600. The bus was two hours late. We shook and swayed and froze all the way to San Antonio arriving at dark 0430 Thursday morning. Carol's walker arrived on the bus. One bag arrived Thursday afternoon and the other finally made it on Friday afternoon. So much for Greyhound and leaving the driving (and the bags) to them.

I asked about the luggage checking system. Once they give you a claim tag they have no record of which bus it goes on, where it comes off, or who picks it up.

Mississippi River Bridge

Altogether it was a good trip. With the exception of the bus ride there were no major catastrohies and lots of good food. Maybe we should try to get back to New Orleans before another 25 years roll by.

Carl Lahser, June, 2013

Elderhostel Christmas in New York
Carl Lahser

In case anybody is interested in an Elderhostel excursion here is the way ours went.

An e-mail listing for an Elderhostel program on Christmas in New York City and the Hudson River Country Mansions sounded interesting. Tuesday through Sunday (6 -11 Dec 05) at the Warwick Conference Center near Warwick, NY. Listed were two day trips to NYC for the Rockettes, the Nutcracker Suite, and window shopping, two day trips along the Hudson River to see Christmas decorations at several old mansions, and classes on Christmas music and the decorations at the mansions.

Reservations were made ($600 each) to Newark (American Airlines, one frequent flyer and one $226.80) and arranged for transportation (Newark to Warwick $95 each).

We were at the airport in San Antonio about 0630 on 6 Dec. Take off was on time (0755) into a clear sky. Near the Illinois border we hit clouds and every thin spot showed snow on the ground. We landed at O'Hare with 45 minutes to make connections. There was about an inch of snow. The next leg was over Indiana and south of Toledo. Lake Erie was to the north with clouds north and south of the lake but no clouds over the lake. Pennsylvania crept under us following US I60 from Youngstown, OH, to Allentown, PA, then across New Jersey to Newark. The weather was clear enough to get a good view of NYC as we landed from the north.

Our Newark arrival was at about 1430 in snow at about 12ºF. We got the bags and waited for another couple due in from California about 1500. Another lady from Toronto joined us for the shuttle ride that left about 1600.

I saw a place selling famous Nathan's hotdogs. I decided to try one. Not bad but $3.89 for a chilidog seems a little high. I killed a Cinnabun with milk for desert. About 2.000 calories.

Our shuttle left a little after 1600. After threading the maze of highways and rush hour traffic we arrived at the Warwick Conference Center about 1730. Temperature was in the lower 30s.

The room was nice with a single and a double bed. Good heat. No TV or clock or phone.

Supper was at 1830 followed by orientation and introductions at 1930. Forty-two attendees from 17 states and Canada.

It was dark a little after 1700. The sky was clear and a quarter moon was near overhead.

Wednesday morning was in the teens with about 6 inches of new powdery snow. It continued to snow most of the day.

Breakfast was at 0800. Pan cakes. At 0900 we had a slide show and talk on the Hudson Valley mansions by Tom Daley. At 1045 we had a class on Christmas music by Betty Venator. I probably learned a couple quantum levels about music in general since I was not taught music back in them ancient days when I was in grade school.

After lunch of pirogues or sour kraut and sausage we had free time until 1600 with nothing planned. We got together with another couple with a car and went to the Hamlet of Sugarloaf. This small community was sort of an artist colony with art galleries, boutiques, and shops selling candles, handicrafts, leather, etc. After about an hour we went back to the Village of Warwick to see what was available. I shot pictures of several churches and homes and stopped in the two book shops. We arrived back at the Center about 1530.

At 1600 we had a talk by Sybil Groff, a New York City native and guide, on the Christmas sights and traditions in NYC. Interesting. Maybe we will get to see some of this.

After supper of turkey and dressing we had more on what to see in NYC. The schedule was changed to go to NYC Thursday to see the Rockettes and the "Christmas Spectacular" at Radio City. This was followed by a two hour walking tour to see Christmas windows and other landmarks. Then to the 1800 show of the "Nutcracker" at Lincoln Center. It was all interesting but cold and tiring. We were back at the Center about 2130. So much for seeing NYC.

Thursday morning we were up for breakfast at 0700 and then got on the bus. It was 19 and clear with about a foot of snow.

Snow covered roofs showed which buildings were occupied and which had good insulation. All the low spots had a crop of Phragmites sticking out of the snow. Roads and parking lots had already been plowed.

Holstein cows in the snow blowing smoke. Farms with barns and silos. Houses dressed for Christmas. Everything looks pretty and new with a coating of snow to cover the real world (real estate sales people called it sellers weather when many defects were covered in snow). A few red oaks with leaves still attached indicating there had been a sudden freeze. A few pines. Sparrows, starlings, crows and a Red-tailed hawk. Gulls.

Lots of traffic. The Holland tunnel. Broadway. Hell's Kitchen. Rockefeller Center. We stopped at the Christmas tree near the skating rink and went into Radio City to see the 1100 show. Rockettes. 3-D Santa. Ice skating scene. Nativity with live camels and donkeys. More Rockettes with a Nutcracker scene. Very good. Complicated stage work. I got a number of natural light shots for our seats in the third balcony. Turned out well with the zoom.

Lunch was not memorable. The walking tour was like many tours where the guide cannot be heard well. St Paul's cathedral. The International Building. Helmsley Towers. We took off on our own to look at windows. Cartier. Bergdorf-Goodman. DeBeers. Trump Towers. Newspaper stands. Hotdog carts. Crowds.

We made it back to the bus and rode up Broadway to Lincoln Center for the 8PM show of the NYC Ballet "Nutcracker". Very well done.

Back on the bus about 10PM for the trip back. Box lunch supper.

We had more snow overnight with a gusting wind. Snow blowing off the roofs. Another schedule change due to weather. More slides and music. Eggs Benedict.

Saturday morning we were up for breakfast (bacon and eggs) and on the bus at 0945. It is clear and cold and the snow is up to the frame of the cars. More pictures of houses along the way. Through Florida, NY, where William Seward (Alaskan Purchase) was born. Up I 87 and across the Hudson River near Rhinebeck and the 2800 acres called Aster Flats (The Asters). A tour of the Mills mansion (He made his money in the California Gold Rush and left trust to maintain the house). Drapes closed to protect the fabrics, paintings, and such. Kids sledding downhill towards the Hudson River.

Off to Hyde Park where the Roosevelt's lived then down the river to the Vanderbilt estate (Fredrick not Commodore Cornelius). Now a National Historic Site. Fredrick made his fortune in railroads, mines, shipping, etc.

On to Poughkeepsie to see the Morris estate, Locust Grove. Samuel Morris was a painter but made his fortune from patent rights for inventing the telegraph.

It was dark when we left and about 1900 when we got back to the Center.

Sunday morning we packed up and had another music class. A sundial in the yard was covered with a foot of snow with the point of the blade sticking out. Guess the time was half past a snow drift. I shot 221 pictures for the trip.

We headed for the Newark airport about 1230 for a 1600 flight to Dallas and San Antonio. The plane was two hours late so we had to stay overnight in Dallas. We were on the 0630 flight to San Antonio on Monday and home by 0900.

Cheese Steak, Anyone?

Cheese Steak, Anyone?
Philadelphia, PA

Carol decided that she wanted to visit Philadelphia. We had a "free" companion flight (for only $99) that had to be used by 30 Jun 2012. She made hotel reservations and we would leave in three days. This is not enough time to do my usual locality research. I had not been there in 25 years since I had had a two-week Naval Reserve assignment at NAS Willowgrove.

Up, up, and away.

We left after lunch on Wednesday, 16 May, an hour and 40 minutes late. We missed our connecting flight in Atlanta and arrived in Philadelphia about midnight. We arrived at the hotel about 0100.

The Crown Plaza West hotel was not the downtown Crown Plaza hotel. It was half an hour by $20 taxi or an hour by $2 bus from the city center. We also found that the special room rate did not include breakfast. Shame on Expedia.

On the way to the hotel Wednesday night we had come along the river on the west side and seen a number of houses along the river all lit up. This morning we were on the other side of the Schuylkill River and the road was blocked off as they prepared for boat races with the long racing shells. Vendor and team tents lined the river.

Thursday was cool, about 60°. We caught the hotel shuttle to the visitor's center downtown and bought a 4-day on/off ticket on the Big Bus. (A company had bought about 200 red double-decked busses from London when London's bus fleet was modernized. They operate several franchises in major cities in the US and Canada.)

I found that riding upstairs was not romantic. It was chilly and not well suited for taking pictures. Historic cities like Philadelphia have progressed over the past 200 years and many of the historic sites have been demolished, moved, or are crowded in between or behind modern structures. Street trees, pedestrians, parked cars and other obstructions prohibit decent meaningful pictures. I found years ago that buying a set of historic site pictures was usually the best bet. These canned pictures are shot in good weather with no obstructions and often include historic views before modern renovations and obstructions. Belligerent drivers don't help either.

We took the hour and a half sightseeing tour and got off for lunch. The bus driver recommended **Sonny's Cheesesteak**. A cheesesteak is thinly sliced beef or chicken with grilled onions smothered in Cheezwhiz in a French roll. I was not greatly impressed.

We walked over to the visitor's center and then to the Independence Center for a historic monologue.

It was getting late and cool so we caught bus No. 33 back to our hotel. One cheap adventure I have had in several big cities has been to catch a bus downtown and ride it to the end of the world and back. Philadelphia. St Louis. Los Angeles. Downtown with old and new buildings and often crowded streets. An industrial zone. Housing from high class to slums with a few abandoned or burned out buildings, churches with bars on the windows. Maybe a few barricaded shops. Out to the suburbs with new houses and shopping centers.

Friday we went to the hotel buffet for breakfast. I asked the cook if he could make a jelly omelet. He said he had never heard of one but then he had never eaten a peanut butter and jelly sandwich either. It was good. I asked if he had heard of chips and gravy —French fries covered in gravy. He said they were called gravy fries in Philly.

We took a bus to town and caught the Red Bus to the Rodin Museum but found the museum closed for renovations. The driver did not mention this.

The Thinker

Gate to Hades

Front Entrance

Something new for me was the "Big Belly Compactors". This was a large square plastic trashcan with a solar cell panel under a Plexiglas dome that powered a garbage compactor. Sounds like a good idea but will they endure? There were also trailer mounted food carts selling Falafel, Cheese steaks, etc.

Falafel Stand

We reboarded the bus and jumped off at the Philadelphia Museum of Art. The museum was built on/in the former water treatment plant reservoir. Lots of good displays. My favorites were the Juan Miro paintings and the Indian temple and artifacts. Near the front entrance to the museum is a statue of Rocky and the stairs he ran up and down for training.

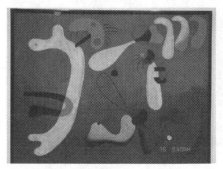

Miro   Indian Art

A shuttle took us to the museum annex where most of the exhibits were fabrics or clothing. The building was an old art deco insurance company home office with lots of carvings and brass work.

Crocheted Annex Entrance   Fabric Arts Display

Next, the bus dropped us at the old Redding Railroad terminal. This was one of the railroads named in the game of Monopoly. The block-square site was closed for several years but has reopened and is now filled with restaurants like a giant food court. We stopped for an ice cream cone and then Carol picked an Amish stand that had rib sandwiches.

Market at old Redding Railroad Terminal

It was after 5PM so we took a bus home. Watching the bus drivers is interesting. In Los Angeles a black driver stopped for blacks politely but for browns or whites she stopped the bus with the door straddling a power pole or sign post. The Philly bus drivers must have been the school bullies since the bus had only two speeds – stop or go fast. The drivers averaged running five yellow lights and one red light per trip.

On Saturday morning we took the bus downtown to see the Franklin Institute. I had hoped for more of a historical theme but it was largely a science demonstration center.

Later, the bus dropped us off on "antique row". The driver had mentioned that the economy had hurt the art and antique business and he was right. Most were out of business or closed for Saturday afternoon.

A taxi took us to McCormick and Schmidt seafood restaurant for a late lunch. We had eaten at this chain in Seattle and Portland and found them very good. They are part of the Landry chain. I had grilled salmon and Carol had fish and chips. We walked a couple blustery blocks to catch the bus for home.

Sunday morning about 1100 we talked to a former city employee as we waited for the bus. She talked about the changes to the city over the previous 25 years. She was not sure all the changes were for the best.

The weather had been clear and cool all week – cool enough for me to wear a jacket. Contrails were visible in a clear blue sky being blown to the north. This indicated a warm front approaching from the south.

We got off at the visitors center and picked up tickets for Independence Hall. The visitor's center sponsored a "Breakfast with Ben" on Sunday mornings that included an hour and a half monologue presentation. We walked to Independence Hall and stopped to look at the Liberty Bell. We stood in line waiting for our time group to enter for their presentation.

This area had changed greatly due to urban renewal. The visitors center grounds covered about four blocks of open area that had been downtown. The Liberty Bell was indoors and roped off. It used to be in Independence Hall and accessible to the public. I patted the bell and probably left my DNA as proof. There were no presentations for the numerous tourists and school groups.

Independence Hall   Liberty Bell

A taxi took us to "the Wok", a Chinese restaurant, for a late lunch. Good food. We walked a couple blocks to the bus stop under clouds and a light mist.

I guess we are getting old. Nightlife consisted of a little TV and a crash. There was nothing but the hotel bar within sight anyway.

Monday it was pack-up-and-go-home time. The weather was drizzly in the 60s. We had a smooth ride to Memphis and San Antonio. Home again.

Carl Lahser
25 May 2012

It was hot in Portland

29 July-4 August 2009

CARL LAHSER

It was hot in Portland

29 July-4 August 2009

CARL LAHSER

We had earned a free airline ticket so Carol decided we should go somewhere. She picked Portland, Oregon, and, since I had not been to Portland for maybe 15 years, I agreed.

The last time I had been in Portland was in early spring when the sky was hazy, the wind damp, and everything was brilliant green. Since this trip would be in late summer I expected it to be a little drier and warmer. Historic weather for July was 58-83°F with 80% humidity and 10 miles visibility. Jumping ahead a little we left San Antonio at 102° and arrived in Portland at a record 103° and had 100°+ for the whole week with haze. On 4 August Portland was expected to have a high of 95° with San Antonio still over 100°. I could have traded a light jacket for more sunscreen.

Wednesday, 29 July. We flew on Delta in a short people airplane (CRJ or Canadian Regional Jet) to Salt Lake City. We left San Antonio an hour late because one of the emergency oxygen units fell open. A maintenance guy tried duct tape but it would not hold so they finally moved the people and left it to swing in the breeze. I guess this proves that this plane was not held together with duct tape.

Salt Lake had a dark brown smog layer. The Great Salt Lake water was Technicolor from blue-green alga in the south and pink halophytic bacteria and protozoa in the north with green marsh grasses in the shallows.

We had a two-hour layover in Salt Lake. The next leg to Portland was on a 767 that was also late. We crossed the Great Salt Lake and across miles of center pivot irrigated fields in Idaho to the Oregon border. There was a big empty lava field with a few dry land farms until we got into the Great Salt Lake coastal mountains. The Columbia River trailed along the Washington border.

We took a $28 taxi downtown and arrived at the hotel at 1300 local time. The room was not ready. We went to lunch and were back at 2PM but the room was still not ready and would not be ready until after 3PM.

We went out and took the Trimet train to Old Town to find Powell's Books. We walked several blocks through where China Town was supposed to be and found that the property had appreciated and Chinese had been priced out and moved. The high taxes had also helped run them out. The buildings had been gutted and turned into high priced condos and shops. The local historic preservation commission required maintaining the façades of old iron work and brick. The walk across town gave the impression of abandoned buildings and homeless people with the hundred year old buildings and people sitting or lying on the sidewalks in any shade available in the 100°+ heat.

We spent an hour in Powell's Books. I was a little disappointed not finding some old books I wanted. The stock was mostly end lots of a few copies of mostly modern books. There were no bargains. We took the train back to the hotel arriving about 5 PM.

The Trimet transportation was free in the central circle that included Old Town. This included rapid transit trains and electric and diesel busses. There was senior seating, wheelchair accessibility, and inside bicycle racks since Portland is a big bicycle town. San Antonio has been debating trolley service for years.

Carol had made a reservation at the Double Tree for a suite with a Jacuzzi. The lip of the Jacuzzi was waist high with no ladder or other means of access and about four feet deep. Carol went to the management and got a regular room without a Jacuzzi for half the price. From a safety viewpoint, the Jacuzzi looked like an accident waiting to happen. It was in violation of at least three major OSHA safety regulations I can think of.

I crashed for a couple of hours, and we went out for supper. The coffee shop had nothing we wanted, so we went to a Quiznos.

Thursday, 30 July. Next morning we hit the hotel dining room for their buffet and made a reservation for a city tour.

About 10AM we caught a train to shop at the Pioneer Courthouse Square. We stopped at the Fossil Cartel shop where Carol bought a ring with a middle Cambrian (500 million year old) trilobite (<u>Elrathia</u> <u>kingi</u>) from Utah (Darn near as old as me!) and some turquoise ear rings. We walked around the mall. She stopped at several shops to look and bought a Kate Spade purse (?) for 70% off. We stopped at the food court for lunch.

We returned to the hotel for a city tour that crisscrossed the city for a couple hours ending the day at the Pittock mansion. The guide explained some of the history and pointed out buildings and neighborhoods of significance. We found that Portland had been divided into a number of neighborhoods with the new area with hotels and the convention centers. We passed the Oregon Zoo, the World Forestry Center and Museum, and Japanese garden, the Classical Chinese Garden, and made stops at the International Rose Test Garden and the Pittock mansion.

Pittock Mansion

The Pittock Mansion, a 16,000 square foot, 30 room mansion, was on a 1000 foot hilltop that overlooked the Willamette River (Wil-LAM-ette dammit as Portlanders say.) It cost the pioneer publisher about $500,000 to build in 1914 but would probably cost that much a year to maintain today. Pittock's children tried to sell the property with no takers and then threatened to demolish it. The neighbors bought it as a museum.

We got dropped off from the tour at McCormick and Schmick's Seafood Restaurant for supper. We had a nice outside table overlooking the river. Carol had a steak, and I had half dozen local oysters, a margarita and salmon stuffed with Dungeness crab.

After supper we got on the wrong train going the wrong way. The driver pointed out on the map where we were and where we wanted to go. We were out of Indian Territory in about half an hour.

Friday, 31 July. Next morning we went to the new Chinese Garden that had opened in 2000. It was built in partnership with Portland's sister city, Suzhou, near Shanghai. It had all the classical Chinese features based on the Ming dynasty gardens. Total cost was about $12.8 million. It is really outstanding particularly since it is manned by volunteers.

Classical Chinese Garden

Leaving the garden we found the Old Town Pizza for lunch. This was where the Portland Underground Walking Tour gathered. The pizza was nothing to brag about but the tour was pretty good.

We had a few minutes before the tour so we went to the Monkey and the Rat, a store selling world-wide antiques and hand crafts. I resisted buying anything but found the potential prices for a lot of my stuff.

The walking tour started in the pizzeria's basement. Many miles of tunnels had been built to allow delivery of merchandise during wet weather. The tunnels were also used as shortcuts between buildings, for storm water drainage, and as utility conduits including the 600 volt lines for the street cars. Pilferage from the businesses and fear that that the tunnels would collapse with the trolley traffic led the businesses and the city to fill in the tunnels that passed under the streets.

The tour passed the Merchants Hotel built for legitimate travelers and past the Barracuda that had been one of the most notorious bars in the Northwest. There were numerous other hotels known as cribs and bars that were famous worldwide for kidnapping or Shanghaiing farmers and lumberjacks to work on the sailing ships - a long interesting history for another time.

We swung down by the river to see the seawall that now keeps Portland from flooding. There was a paddle wheeler belonging to the museum open for visitors. This was the reason shanghaiing stopped in 1896 - steam ships came into common use that needed 8 engineers who could read rather than 28 warm bodies.

Voodoo Donut

We passed the Voodoo Doughnut Shop and tried one of their special voodoo donuts. It was a jelly-filled with arms and eyes painted on its head. It was served with pretzel sticks so you could cast a voodoo spell.

On the way back to the hotel I saw an overweight man sitting on a bus bench rocking back and forth like an autistic. I had never before seen an autistic adult out by himself.

There were not many birds. A group of swallows or swifts cruised mid river. A young blue jay screamed for mama. A few pigeons and sparrows were in the parks. Several crows appeared separately along with a few Canadian geese along the river mud flats.

Back at the hotel we made reservations for the Ringside, one of the "top ten steak restaurants in the country". It was so dark they provided flashlights to see the menu. The steak was good but I seldom go for $40 meals.

Saturday, 1 August. We left about 0900 for the Saturday Market. This was near Skidmore Fountain in Riverside Park. The Tri-Met train took us from the hotel past the two spires of the Oregon Convention Center, near Rose Quarter Arena and across the Steel Bridge. Columns of insects, probably midges, were suspended in mid river drifting with the breeze.

Opening time was 10AM but many vendors were setup and ready to go. There were portrait artists including one who made clay portraits.

Caricature Artist

Many craftsmen worked in wood and glass. One sold squashed glass bottles. Some sold custom clothing. Numerous food booths sold ice cream, Polish, Greek, Japanese and other ethnic foods.

We went to the Lloyd Center mall about a block from the hotel. It had a couple hundred shops, a food court, and an ice rink. Later in the evening we went to Stanford's Restaurant in the mall. It had very good food at much more reasonable prices.

Sunday, 2 August. We had reservations for the Columbia River and Mount Hood tour for all day Sunday. They picked us up about 10:30. We drove through town to US84 and headed east along the Columbia River.

The river had cut through giant lava flows on its way to the sea. The canyon walls were striated with the numerous flows over time. There was some boat and barge traffic taking lumber to the mills.

First stop was at Wahkenna Falls about 30 miles from Portland. It dropped 242 feet. Half a mile further we stopped at Multnomah Falls that drops 611 feet. There was a visitor center and snack shop near the road. There was a bridge crossing the pool at the bottom.

Wahkenna Falls   Multnomah Falls

Vegetation, besides big trees, included Cranes Bill, Kininik, Woods Strawberry, Horsetails, Fireweed, Wandering Fleabane, Solomon's seal, and Hawkweed. Further up Mt Hood there were masses of Broadleaf Lupine.

Three miles further was Horsetail Falls that drops 176 feet. There was a sign and a parking lot. Ponytail Falls was across the road and about a half a mile downhill.

Horsetail Falls

Hood River Windsurfing

We stopped at the Federal Fish Hatchery where they raised rainbow trout and sturgeon. The hatchery operation was over for the year. A few miles further east was the little town of Hood River famous for wind surfing. There were a number of different styles working the surf. We had lunch as we watched the activity on the river. Wind surfing. Kite surfing. Balloon surfing. Anything that would propel a surfboard.

Lunch was good. I had a salad with a microbrewed beer.

After lunch we turned south down state highway 35 towards Mt Hood. There were scattered farms mixed with forest. Crops included plums, pears, peaches, cherries, and grapes. This was also a wine country.

We turned onto a park road that led to the Timberline Lodge. The 55,000 square foot structure was built on Mt. Hood in 1937 by the WPA. It sits at 6000 feet about half way up the eastern face of the 11,245 foot mountain. This was built as a ski lodge and retreat and is the site of numerous weddings.

Mt. Hood

We went back to the bottom and drove through farming country and through Gresham on the way back home. We made a fruit stop where I bought some delicious cherries and a couple of so-so peaches.

Supper was at a Chinese/Thai restaurant that was ok but did not do a real good job of either countries food

Monday, 3 August. We went back to old town and stopped at the Bijou for breakfast. Carol said it was supposed to be "trendy" and since it took over 30 minutes to get served I guess it met the requirement.

We shopped some more and went over to the river to catch a boat ride. We found the only ride available when we were there was a two hour trip 12 miles up the Willamette River aboard the "Spirit". This part of the river is totally developed with luxury homes, hundreds of house boats, a golf course and country club. There is also one of the city water pumping stations.

There were a couple of real art galleries on the way to the hotel. Good work at high prices.

We returned to the hotel and made reservations at Jake's Crawfish Restaurant. This was another "world famous" eatery. It was good but I was disappointed because they had no crayfish. This reminded me of the old Australian ballad about the pub with no beer. Since there were no crayfish I had a wedge salad with "baby" shrimp that were really freshwater <u>Paleomonetes</u> or glass shrimp and a Corona.

As a side note, there was a plague on European crayfish beginning in Italy about 1860. It rapidly spread north through France and Germany to Sweden and recently into England and Turkey.

The disease was identified as the fungus Aphanomyces astaci. Researchers found that the source was imported live North American crayfish including the local Northwestern Signal Crayfish (Pacifiasticus leniusculus). Although this crayfish is resistant to the fungus it is a carrier. It is also more aggressive than most European crayfish and either killed or interbred with the European crayfish producing sterile hybrids.

The EU has banned importation of live US crayfish. Not only have the foreign crayfish introduced and spread a fatal fungus to the native population, they have also disrupted the host community, reduced biological diversity, disrupted the host environment and community, and provided a permanent source of spores for plague fungus. This in turn has caused a reduction in fish stocks and slowed growth of local fisheries, changed the diet of indigenous mammals and birds, and had negative commercial implications within Europe.

Tuesday, 4 August. We were up about 0400 to pack and catch a taxi at 0500 to hurry out to the airport for a 0705 plane. The plane was a half hour late due to a glitch in the computer seating program. The last leg of the trip was on another short people plane, the only one of the four planes on time. We were in good ole hot San Antonio by mid afternoon.

Remarks.
  1.   Portland and suburbs has a population of about 2.5 million.

2. Oregon has no sales tax but it does have high property taxes and an income tax.
3. Portland is actually on the Willamette River about six miles from the Columbia.
4. The seawall protection for the business district did not extend to cover the slummy River District. In one flood hundreds of buildings disappeared and an unknown number drowned. The official number drowned is about 200. Many were probably washed miles downstream.
5. There were about 70 miles of tunnels that connected the basements of most of the businesses along the first couple block inland along the river. They were built to deliver merchandise without getting it wet from the frequent rains. They were also used for drainage, ventilation, and utility corridors.
6. Portland was racially proactive. The Japanese population which once owned much of Old Town was locked up within hours of the attack on Pearl Harbor. In the 1950s, a rich Japanese man named Naito bought back much of the former Japanese property that appreciated making him a bundle.
7. Portland has a long history of discrimination. Portland has few Blacks or Jews and a long association with the KKK.

Santa Fe Get Away

Santa Fe Getaway 04

Introduction. This trip began in the fall of 2003 when our local public TV station offered a "Santa Fe Getaway" as a fundraiser. After some discussion we decided on mid-April, 2004. We received the voucher and discovered the trip would cover only three nights mid-week. From a Pollyanna viewpoint this abbreviated trip would allow a variety of activities. We could cover galleries in Albuquerque, Santa Fe, Taos and surroundings, and see a couple pueblos. It would be a few weeks early for the best birds and wild flowers but should be interesting.

We flew on the Southwest cattle car flight to Albuquerque on Monday, 5 April 2004. It was $99 plus taxes for each of us each way. We landed at 1100 (11 AM), rented a car and drove to Santa Fe.

It was cooler and wetter than I had ever seen New Mexico. According to the weather guessers this equaled the record low temperature and exceeded the annual moisture for the past century. I'm not too thrilled about lows in the 30's but the highs would be in the 50's. Tolerable. The desert after a rain is the most beautiful it can get and in another couple weeks the desert would explode in wildflowers. The color of the wet rocks and hills is intense. The area had been in a drought for several years and this rain and snowfall would help.

Lunch was in Bernalillo at Abuellitas restaurant for a New Mexican lunch. The galleries were open on weekends only and the one antique store was terribly overpriced.

I had not been to Santa Fe for more than supper in maybe twenty years. Along the road to Santa Fe several casinos had been built on the First Nation Reservations along the highway and the highway had been improved. Much of the range was still overgrazed and the drought had not helped. Homes on the Reservations near the casinos now looked like any other homes off the Reservations. When I first came through this area about 40 years back the reservation homes were small adobe structures or trailer houses each with a giant TV antenna and a pickup truck. Many Reservation homes still looked that way.

Our hotel reservations at the Marriott Courtyard were for Tuesday thru Thursday nights so we found a bed and breakfast, called *Inn on the*

Paseo, near downtown on Paseo de Peralta. By the time we arrived and moved in downtown was already closed at 1700 (5 PM).

Highway Albuquerque to Santa Fe

We walked down Palace St. past the St. Francis Cathedral and the Indian Arts Museum looking in the windows of galleries and other stores

Sunset turns adobe gold

around the plaza. We passed the historic La Fonda Hotel and the Joe Wade gallery with their huge outdoor bronzes while on our way to the Loretto Chapel. By then it was getting dark with a spectacular sunset that turned the adobe a many shades of gold.

Golden sunset

The temperature went down with the sun. Carol stopped and bought a genuine handmade imitation alpaca jacket from Bolivia.

The route home was up Washington with supper at the Inn of the Anasazi hotel. We passed the library and the newspaper and crashed for the night about 2200 (10 PM). The 7000-foot altitude hit me harder than it used to.

Tuesday morning we were up and at the breakfast table about 0800. There was no hurry since few things downtown opened before 1000. I hauled everything down to the car and about 0930 we began walking over to the O'Keefe Museum. Temperature was about 40°F. There was a clear blue sky but the airliners were leaving long contrails.

Texas Mulberry trees (<u>Morus</u> <u>microphyla</u>) were leafing out. Scattered forsythia was in bloom. Flowerbeds looked straggly with only one or two tulips, hyacinths, or daffodils blooming at a time. More plants were getting ready to bloom. Santa Fe is 60 miles north and 1000 feet higher than Albuquerque so spring comes about two weeks later.

Carol stopped to rest in front of the convention center. I went to see the visitors' bureau but the person was on a terminal phone call with her back to me. I left and walked to the Georgia O'Keefe museum. When Carol arrived we bought tickets and toured the gallery. The tour began with a biographical movie. I had known little about her and had seen only a few of her pictures. Outstanding.

We left and toured several galleries. One had oriental and Latin American antiques. Very interesting.

O'Keefe Museum

As we passed the Fine Arts museum I saw a Western Kingbird (Tyrannus verticalis) glide into a pine flashing its black tail.

Sidewalk Vendors

I also heard a wren that sounded much like a house wren with two low, slow notes on the end. Canyon Wren (<u>Catherpes</u> <u>mexicanus</u>)?

Carol had to look at the Indian silver on display around the plaza. Two blocks of vendors had their wares spread out on blankets on the sidewalk and she only skipped a few. I went to pick up the car and come back for her.

On the way back to the car I stopped at the Indian Arts Museum for a book on identifying and dating potshards but no luck. I also stopped at Nicholas Potter bookseller. Again not luck.

We drove to East de Vargas to see the oldest house still standing. The street was narrow and one-way. We crossed the Old Santa Fe Trail and found a parking place near the oldest house and the San Miguel Mission. Although there was a pueblo on the site dating to 1250 AD the continuity is questionable. As for the mission it was burned during the Pueblo Revolt and had been totally rebuilt.

Oldest House in US

We headed out to the Marriott Courtyard motel and checked in. Looking at the restaurant information we decided to go to the Coyote Cafe at 1900 (7 PM). We drove down to the plaza and about three times around the area to find a parking place. The Coyote was an outstanding place to eat. My scallops and pilaf was a gastronomic orgasm. Carols steak was very good. No native dishes on the menu.

Wednesday morning we had the hotel breakfast buffet and headed north to Espanola. The first few miles were under construction until we hit US 84/285. I stopped to take pictures of Camel Rock in between the traffic.

We thought about stopping at pueblos along the way. The Tesuque pueblo was closed. The San Ildefonso pueblo was a big gas station and "smoke shop" with tax-free cigarettes.

Camel Rock

We arrived in Espanola and circled through town looking for galleries or antique shops. The only ones in town opened on weekends. So much for Espanola. The town is famous for old cars and car shows. We saw none. The visitor center had a lot of information on the area.

Route 76 took us towards Chimayo. We stopped at several shops along the road. I was amazed at the cost of blankets and silver. I was in the area about forty years ago and prices had increased ten to fifteen times with some blankets that would have sold for $80 now over $1000.

One shop had all hand carved items. While Carol browsed I looked outside at their plum and apple trees and heard a strange bird. I finally saw it – a Mexican Grackle (<u>Cassidix</u> <u>mexicanus</u>). The shop owner, a

Pueblo lady, said it came back every year and sat in the top of the Pinyon pine (<u>Pinus</u> <u>edulis</u>) and sang to her. I had never thought of grackle sound as singing but yes.

We drove through the town of Chimayó and were looking for the historic Santuario de Chimayó. This is the local version of Lourdes and pilgrims walk there from miles around along the highways. The proper intersection was not well marked so we missed it.

A mile or so later we saw a gallery of bronze statues. The farm also bred rare animals especially donkeys. The bronzes were well done.

We found the right road and finally passed a large number of parked cars of people getting the church ready for Easter and decided not to interfere. Another reason was the closest parking was half a mile down the road.

Back up the road we stopped at the Restaurante Rancho de Chimayó. I had a relleno made in a sopapea that covered the plate and was too much to finish. Carol had a combination New Mexico plate. The restaurant is an old ranch house built on three levels up the hillside.

Continuing down the road we visited the San Juan Pueblo. There were a number of willow trees near the Rio Grande River below the confluence with the Chama River. In the trees were a collection of one and two story Pueblo-style houses, a rebuilt church, an admin building, a post office, and the Oke Oweence Arts and Crafts Cooperative. We shopped the co-op and bought a few things.

I talked with one of the women in the co-op who was well versed on the invasive species like Russian olive and Salt Cedar. I was not surprised but just had not expected the discussion. She said there was no money for invasive plant control.

We drove back to Espanola stopping a moment to take pictures of the Chama River. Back on Highway 84 we headed northwest up the Chama River to Abiquiú where Georgia O'Keefe had lived. We passed Pedernal, a butte O'Keefe had painted several times, and turned at a sign that said library. After driving a couple miles of rough road and passing some unimpressive dwellings the road became a private road to the O'Keefe hacienda. Not much of a town.

Continuing up Hwy 84 there were a lot of buttes and walls of banded red and yellow rock. The rain made the colors stand out. I stopped to shoot some of the rock formations and rain clouds over the Abiquiú Reservoir.

San Juan Pueblo

Butte called Pedernal

Fourteen miles further north was Ghost Ranch where Georgia O'Keefe had also painted. We turned in and visited the cultural and archeological museums and the bookstores. There is a two-week archeological field school every August after the monsoon.

Back on Hwy 84 we continued north passing the Echo Amphitheatre a natural aeolian blowout. We continued up to the small farming town of Tierra Amarilla. The town was located in a pretty valley. Similar wide shallow valleys are called Parks in Colorado and Utah. Cattle and fruit trees.

Echo Amphitheatre

We headed east on Hwy 64 through the San Juan Mountains and the Carson National Forest for 48 uninhabited miles to Tres Piedras. We began seeing Pinyon pine (<u>Pinus</u> <u>edulis</u>) on the hills, then beside and then below us. Quaking Aspen (<u>Populus</u> <u>tremuloides</u>) was mixed with pines on hillsides. Common Juniper (<u>Juniperus</u> <u>communis</u>) and small oaks with the dead leaves still on that looked like Gambel Oak (<u>Quercus</u> <u>gambellii</u>) were along the road. Gambel Oak grows in thickets from root sprouts. We used to joke that there was probably only one tree with roots covering west Texas, New Mexico, Colorado and parts of Arizona.

Painted Rocks

Then we noted snow under the trees, then big drops of rain, then snow. Temperature dropped from 51°F to 32°F. Once over the pass the snow stopped and intermittent rain began. Several small flocks of Lincoln's Sparrows (<u>Melospiza</u> <u>lincolnii</u>) flew at shin height across the road.

After crossing Hwy 285 we were in sagebrush another 30 miles and across the Rio Grande Gorge Bridge to Taos. The weather was cool with intermittent rain all the way. It was after 1700 and everything was closed. The Taos pueblo was closed for the season. We passed through town on Hwy 68. It was up and down the steep curving river road through Pilar and Embudo to Espanola. It was after sundown and it rained all the way along Hwy 84 to the hotel.

Snow in April

Rain coming

Thursday morning we got up, gassed up and drove through snow and spitting rain to Taos. By the time we arrived blue sky was showing above the mountains to the west. A pair of Black-billed Magpies (<u>Pica</u> <u>pica</u>) flew across the road.

We stopped at the Taos visitor center. There was a junior art show going on and even the kids wanted several hundred bucks for good stuff.

Since the city was redoing the city parking lot I was told to park behind the Catholic Church. The rain had slacked off and patches of blue were showing overhead as we walked to the plaza. We looked at every gallery around the plaza, a block east on Kit Carson Rd. and most north on N. Pueblo Rd. Many interesting pieces. The best galleries in my estimation were the Variant Gallery and Gallery A. Like Santa Fe and Albuquerque the real galleries were fewer than in the past and there were more souvenir shops.

It was after noon when we decided to look for lunch. The only Native American restaurant listed in Taos was out the road to the pueblo past the casino. It appeared to be out of business. Along the road was a big willow in new yellow foliage against the backdrop of the snowy mountains crowned by snow clouds. I could have been skiing.

A lone Black Vulture (<u>Coragyps</u> <u>atratus</u>) cruised against the foot of the mountains looking for an updraft.

Artsy Wet Adobe wall

We stopped at the Woman's Gallery where women had made everything. The owner suggested a small New Mexican place called Antonio's with good food about a mile further north. You can't miss the desert red and blue building with a brush fence. They served avocado pie for dessert – much like key lime pie.

Coming back to town we stopped at an antique shop called Ec Lec Tic that sold Chinese and oriental pieces. Prices were moderate.

The trip back to Santa Fe was punctuated by rain and snow flurries. We stopped along the Rio Grande River and got out in the rain to shoot some pictures.

Snow on the Mountains and a Willow leafing out

Friday morning we packed up and left for Albuquerque. It was a little over an hour's drive. We went to Old Town for a couple hours then out to the airport. We had lunch at the airport Gardinios and waited for the plane to arrive an hour late. We were back home by 9 PM.

Rio Grande River

Native Birds and Plants seen on the trip

It was cold and wet and a couple weeks early for migratory birds and much to be blooming.

Birds
Black Vulture (<u>Coragyps</u> <u>atratus</u>)
Western Kingbird (<u>Tyrannus</u> <u>verticalis</u>)
Black-billed Magpies (<u>Pica</u> <u>pica</u>)
Canyon Wren (<u>Catherpes</u> <u>mexicanus</u>)
Mexican Grackle (<u>Cassidix</u> <u>mexicanus</u>).
Lincoln's Sparrows (<u>Melospiza</u> <u>lincolnii</u>.

Plants
Pinyon pine (<u>pinus</u> <u>edulis</u>)
Common Juniper (<u>Juniperus</u> <u>communis</u>)
Narrowleaf Cottonwood (<u>Populus</u> <u>angustifolia</u>)
Quaking Aspen (<u>Populus</u> <u>tremuloides</u>)
Bebb Willow (<u>Salix</u> <u>bibbiana</u>)
Gooding Willow (<u>Salix</u> <u>gooddingii</u>)
Gambel Oak (<u>Quercus</u> <u>gambellii</u>)
White Mulberry (<u>Morus</u> <u>alba</u>)
Texas Mulberry (<u>Morus</u> <u>microphylla</u>)
Four-wing Saltbush (<u>Atriplex</u> <u>canescens</u>)

Blue Ridge, Georgia

April 2007

by

Carl Lahser

Blue Ridge, Georgia, April 2007

Carl Lahser

4 May 07

We received an e-mail asking if we would be interested in a house swap during Fiesta week, 23-30 April, here in San Antonio for a week in Blue Ridge, GA. We seldom do anything during the Fiesta anyway, and we had never been to that part of the world so we accepted.

Blue Ridge is about 100 miles north of Atlanta at the southern end of the Blue Ridge Mountains. It's near the Copper Basin and the tri-state region where Georgia, Tennessee, and South Carolina meet. It was in the heart of Cherokee country so there was not a big rush to settle the area. Gold was discovered in 1828 nearby in Dahlonega. Mineral springs were a tourist attraction. Not far to the north in the Copper Basin copper was discovered in 1843 near Ducktown. Several rivers and lakes and waterfalls are tourist attractions. Antiques and crafts are abundant.

Sunday. Instead of flying and renting a car we decided to drive the 1100 miles. We would leave early Sunday morning and arrive Monday evening. It did not quite work that way and we finally left the house about 1400 stopping in Lake Charles for the night instead of Biloxi. It rained most of the way to Houston and was cloudy to the Louisiana border.

Monday morning we got on the interstate heading east flying along a hundred-yard wide green tunnel through the woods. Between Beaumont and Cameron were occasional glimpses of commercial crawfish ponds but most of the trip was down this tunnel of trees.

I bought a new toy to use on the trip. This was a Garmin Streetfinder GPS unit. Put in your destination and it tells you the shortest route and details on getting there. It's really good for finding motels, gas stations, and places to eat along the Interstate where you can't see anything along the road. It takes you right to the door. It talks telling you where to turn and recalculates a route in case you miss a turn. It was really good finding the way on the freeways through cities. It also eliminated quite a bit of arguing, and maps flapping across the driver's face. Main problem is is is continuously out of date.

Monday night was spent near Auburn, Alabama, at a Holiday Inn. We filled the car with the highest priced gas of the trip at $2.98/gallon. We were on the road a little after 0900 and turned north a little west of Atlanta for the last hundred miles. Near Blue Ridge we punched in the address and it almost took us to the front door. We missed a couple turns on the winding hilly road even with the help of Expedia maps off the Internet and arrived about 1300 under overcast skies.

The house was wonderful. Three levels. Five bedrooms. Good view to the Cuttlewhee Mountains of Tennessee and North Carolina. Enough acreage to prevent anyone spoiling the view. It was built for a retirement home in a few years.

Home Exchange

The two decks had bird feeders. Tufted Titmouse (<u>Baeolophus</u> <u>bicolor</u>). Carolina Chickadee (<u>Poecile</u> <u>carolinensis</u>). White-breasted Nuthatch (<u>Sitta</u> <u>carolinensis</u>). Male and female Rose-breasted Grosbeak (<u>Pheucticus</u> <u>ludovicianus</u>). Downy Woodpecker (<u>Picoides</u> <u>pubescens</u>). Red-shouldered Hawk (<u>Buteo</u> <u>lineatus</u>). American Goldfinch (<u>Carduelis</u> <u>tristis</u>) at a tall thistle feeder. Ruby-throated Hummingbirds (<u>Archilochus</u>

colubris) at a feeder. Blue Jay (<u>Cyanocitta</u> <u>cristata</u>). Mourning Dove (<u>Zenaida</u> <u>macroura</u>). American Crow (<u>Corvus</u> <u>brachyrhynchos</u>). Brown Thrasher (<u>Toxostoma</u> <u>rufum</u>). Mockingbird (<u>Mimus</u> <u>polyglottus</u>). I had never seen the first six in person before. I also heard a Cardinal (<u>Cardinalis</u> <u>cardinalis</u>), a Northern Flicker (<u>Colaptes</u> <u>auratus</u>), a Red-shouldered Hawk (<u>Buteo</u> <u>lineatus</u>) and a Yellow-billed Cuckoo (<u>Coccyzus</u> <u>americanus</u>). (By Sunday morning it had warmed up and many of the Grosbeaks had departed.)

Rose-breasted Grosbeak

We drove back to Blue Ridge to see the visitor center for local information and to pick up some groceries. The downtown area included a train station and numerous antique shops and galleries.

In for the night, we watched "Heroes" and prepared to crash. Out on the deck it was dark with a half moon directly overhead. There was a thin overcast with Venus showing but no stars. Not a sound could be heard. A few distant lights twinkled through the tree branches.

Wednesday morning we went to see the shops of Blue Ridge. We parked near the Depot on E. Main St. A few places were closed on Wednesday but there were plenty of others to see. Most of the shops sold candles and other tourist stuff. There was one gallery with local oils and several other artists on consignment. One shop of particular interest was called the Cold Creek Trading Company. It advertised Native American Indian art and crafts. Remarkable. Huicol (Mexican Sierra Madre indigenous) made in Malaysia with paint dots instead of beads. Haida and Cree (First Nation western Canada) canoe paddles, masks, and story poles also made in Malaysia. Cocopelli dancers (Hopi and Zuni) of Arizona made in Indonesia. Australian dot art and a Didgeridoo made in Indonesia. The prices for decorator items were inexpensive. Cree paddles for $20. The didgeridoo was only $30.

After lunch at the Blue Ridge Mountain BBQ, we tried one of the self-guiding tours but gave up after nearly getting run over and winding up on roads that lead to someone's cabin.

We drove up to the old mining towns of McCaysville, Georgia and Copperhill, Tennessee. They intermingle and straddle the Tennessee/Georgia state line. Some of the buildings and homes have been restored but most are relatively new.

Ducktown

The Ocoee River flow into town from Georgia, changes its name and leaves into Tennessee as the Toccoa River. We continued up US 68 to Ducktown and stopped at the Bura Bura Mine and Ducktown Basin Museum. A gold prospector discovered copper about 1840. It was developed and produced copper, zinc, iron and sulfur for about a hundred years. The ore was only about 1% copper so more money has been made from sales of sulfuric acid, copper sulfate for fertilizer, and iron.

The Thursday morning rain was first a drizzle and then a hard rain. It rained or was cloudy until about 1600 when the sun came out. Georgia needed the rain.

We drove to town about noon and stopped at the Multitudes Gallery. It specialized in stained glass and blown glass art. They represented some very good artists.

We drove to Cherry Log for lunch at the Pink Pig. Former President Jimmy Carter was reported to have been a patron. The chicken and dumplings entree was not ready, so I ordered a BBQ plate. I forgot we were in the Deep South where picked BBQ is king, or I would have tried something else. I sampled their Brunswick stew. It was more vinegary than I liked. So much for Jimmy Carter's gastronomic palate.

the Pink Pig

Ellijay was the next stop. We visited six antique malls comparing prices with San Antonio. The prices and the variety were about the same. There were more reproductions than we had at home.

One shop was selling willow furniture. I remember seeing willow lawn furniture as a kid. It was not expensive and would often root and grow in the lawn.

Friday morning came up sunny. Mist, locally called smoke, rose out of the valleys. I did the laundry, and we left to catch the train about 0930. The Blue Ridge Scenic Railway travels 13 miles to McCaysville and returns. The route is along the Ocoee River that changes its name when it crosses into Tennessee. Weird. The train left at 1030 and arrived about an hour later.

State Line

We had almost two hours for lunch and shopping before the train headed back. We had lunch at the Nifty 50s restaurant sitting outside along the river. Bank Swallows (<u>Riparia</u> <u>riparia</u>) cruised the river. I had the Elvis special, a grilled peanut and banana sandwich. The Nifty

50s was decorated in red vinyl booths and a black and white tile floor. We visited a couple of antique malls. Carol bought a nice print at a photographer's gallery, and we headed back for the train.

Nifty 50's Café

An item of historic interest was the Cherokee fish trap in the river. It was one of four in the river and was thought to be 300-400 years old. These traps were built similar to the Polynesian and European fish traps.

Cherokee fish trap

We went to supper at the Victorian House Restaurant across from the depot. Good food but moderately expensive.

Saturday was nice weather. We drove to Dahlonega along one of the most crooked roads I had ever driven. The route was mostly through large broadleaf trees with occasional fields and pastures. Some of the houses were huge. We met about a hundred motorcycles on a rally in the area.

We began at the visitor's center (which used to be the city hall) and got directions to the gold mine museum, two goldmine attractions and three waterfalls. The gold mine museum in the county courthouse was our first stop. They had displays of gold and gold mining memorabilia and a movie of interviews with old timers.

The square was interesting with a variety of shops. One major difference was the presence of tasting rooms for three wineries around Dahlongea. A group of musicians had gathered in front of the courthouse and were playing Bluegrass music.

Bluegrass music

After lunch we drove to one of the gold mines. The Consolidated mine had panning for gold and a tour of the renovated mine. The mine opened in 1900 and was mined out by 1906. The next tour was an hour away, so we decided to see the waterfalls and go to Brasstown Bald, the highest point in Georgia.

We found the first waterfall, DeSoto Falls, named for some Spanish armor found near the falls. It was a half-mile walk to the falls through the woods. Trillium and Lady Slipper orchids and pretty little violets were in bloom.

It was another hour's drive to Brasstown Bald. We found the park already closed for the day at 1600. They closed the gate, locked the outhouse, and boogied. There was a ¾ mile moderate walk to the visitor's center on top that Carol thought was excessive.

Brasstown Bald

We drove to the Brasstown Resort near the town of Young Harris for supper. They served an outstanding surf and turf buffet that made up for some of the disappointments of the day.

Sunday morning we did the laundry, made the bed, and restored the house to its original condition. We packed and left about 1000.

Blue Ridge had a craft fair. We stopped on the way out of town. It featured handmade jewelry, wooden toys, honey, jelly and fudge.

It was a nice day for cruising the green tunnel roads, and we were in Panama City, Florida about 1800. The hydrogen sulfide odor from the paper plant was still a prominent feature of the town.

Monday morning I drove out to Tyndall AFB to visit a couple of friends and visit the Tyndall Beach. This beach is on Tyndall AFB and is one of the prettiest beaches on the Gulf Coast. I got a few shells and pictures of Laughing Gulls (<u>Larus</u> <u>atricilla</u>) and Sanderlings (<u>Crocethia</u> <u>alba</u>).

I picked up Carol at the motel about noon, and we headed for San Antonio. About 1900 we stopped for the night in Slidell, LA. About 0330 Tuesday morning we were awakened by the motel management saying our car had been broken into. They had broken the driver's window and stolen our GPS. The GPS was not stuck to the windshield but was sitting on the console between the seats and well lighted by the motel security lights.

Broken Window

The police report and reports to the motel management and our insurance company were complete about 0500. There was no mobile glass service available, so I had the fun of driving home with no window.

Tuesday morning the sky was threatening but we avoided any rain and were home by 1900. It was a good exchange to an interesting and beautiful area of the country.

Birds

Family

Hawks	Red-shouldered Hawk (<u>Buteo</u> <u>lineatus</u>)
Sandpiper	Sanderlings (<u>Crocethia</u> <u>alba</u>)
Gull-Tern	Laughing Gulls (<u>Larus</u> <u>atricilla</u>)
Doves	Mourning Dove (<u>Zenaida</u> <u>macroura</u>)
Cuckoos	Yellow-billed Cuckoo (<u>Coccyzus</u> <u>americanus</u>)
Hummingbirds	Ruby-throated Hummingbirds (<u>Archilochus</u> <u>colubris</u>)
Swallows	Bank Swallow (<u>Riparia</u> <u>riparia</u>)
Jays	Blue Jay (<u>Cyanocitta</u> <u>cristata</u>) American Crow (<u>Corvus</u> <u>brachyrhynchos</u>)
Woodpeckers	Downy Woodpecker (<u>Picoides</u> <u>pubescens</u>) Northern Flicker (<u>Colaptes</u> <u>auratus</u>)
Titmice	Tufted Titmouse (<u>Baeolophus</u> <u>bicolor</u>) Carolina Chickadee (<u>Poecile</u> <u>carolinensis</u>)
Nuthatches	White-breasted Nuthatch (<u>Sitta</u> <u>carolinensis</u>)
Thrashers	Brown Thrasher (<u>Toxostoma</u> <u>rufum</u>)
Mockingbirds	Mockingbird (<u>Mimus</u> <u>polyglottus</u>)
Finches	Rose-breasted Grosbeak (<u>Pheucticus</u> <u>ludovicianus</u>) American Goldfinch (<u>Carduelis</u> <u>tristis</u>)

Las Vegas Spree in 1958

By

Carl Lahser

Las Vegas Spree

I had just turned 22
In the Navy
In California
When with some Navy buddies
One Friday night after a couple beers
Decided we should see Las Vegas

We drove into the sun
Across the desert
From Long Beach
To Barstow
To Las Vegas

About dark we arrived
And found a cheap motel
And drove through town
Las Vegas was empty
By today's standards

We looked around.
The Gold Nugget.
The Golden Dollar.
I took pictures
Until this great big
Cowboy looking fellow
Said, in a low voice,
"We don't shoot
pictures in here, Son."

"Yes Sir. You bet.
I'm out of here,"
says me.

Way late at night
Or was it early next morning
I put a dollar on the roulette wheel
And got a free drink and the free buffet
And still had enough for gas.

It was sunrise when we hoisted the anchor.

And said "Good bye, Las Vegas"

Cruise through the Panama Canal

April 2003

By

Carl Lahser

Cruise through the Panama Canal April 2003

Introduction. Carol came home from bridge one night after discussing vacations with other players and decided she wanted to take a cruise through the Panama Canal. I'm retired so why not. Shortly thereafter an offer of a cruise through the Panama Canal arrived on the computer. She thought it looked like fun so we booked on 8 July 02.

I had been to Panama 35 years before. This was long before Noriega when we still had several Army and Air Force bases and the Panama Canal Company ran the canal. I visited the Miraflores lock and took the train along the Canal. Shopping had been good on both ends of the Canal. I liked the bird watching and seeing the jungle of Central America.

Price quoted was $1399 each plus $279 port charges and tax of $279 each plus cruise insurance of $128 each totaling $3612. This was for one of their 624 ocean view cabins with extended balcony on the Carnival Spirit for a 16-night cruise leaving Miami terminal 3 on Tuesday, 1 April 03.

The ship was gross weight of 86,000 tons and was 893 feet long with 106 feet beam designed for Panama Canal passage. The maximum size ship allowed through the locks is 965 feet by 106 feet beam. The lock chambers are 110 feet by 990 feet. Not much wiggle room.

Itinerary was proposed as: 0800-1400 Friday in Cartagena, Columbia; Panama Canal transit 0800-1600 Saturday; 0800-1800 Monday in Punt Arena, Costa Rica; Acapulco 0700 Thursday to 0400 Friday; 0800-1700 in Puerto Vallarta on Saturday; 0800-1700 Sunday in Mazatlan; 0700-1400 in Cabo San Lucas on Tuesday; and dock in San Diego at 0700 Thursday. We used frequent flyer miles for American Airline electronic tickets from San Antonio to Miami and San Diego to San Antonio. This schedule turned out to be 80-90% correct.

I did my homework on birds and local histories in books and on the Internet. I took *A Guide to the Birds of Venezuela* by de Schauensee and Phelps and *A Field Guide to the Birds of Mexico and Central America* by Irby Davis.

The itinerary looked interesting except I found nothing on Punta Arena specifically. I found the port had closed about ten years previous and had recently reopened along with a new commercial port that was still under construction.

I found a good list of the area birds from one of the resorts. Websites like:

http://www.lonelyplanet.com
http://www.blackworld.com
http://www.mytravelguide.com
http://www.ddg.com
http://www.about.com

had a lot of maps and information. There were several websites with pictures and narrative of similar cruises and a lot of information on the resorts on the Mexican Rivera.

Day 0.

We flew to Miami on 31 Mar from San Antonio at 0840 to DFW and arriving in Miami at 1430. We crossed East Texas and Louisiana hitting the Gulf over the very mouth of the Mississippi River. We were feet dry near Ft Meyers then across the Everglades to Miami. There were more gravel pits than I remembered from the late 70's and Florida International University had grown from two buildings to a large campus. We flew half way to the Bahamas and turned to land from the east.

The weather was cool as we waited for the hotel shuttle to take us to the Wyndham Airport hotel, our designated transfer point.

We checked in for the night and then checked in with the cruise people and were given a schedule for transportation to the port.

Day 1.

Next morning we tagged the bags and got them down for transportation by 1000. We checked out of the hotel ($148.48) and sat around for two hours waiting for transportation. Tipping had begun with the taxi driver from the house, the hotel shuttle driver, the porter, the maid, another porter, the bus baggage handler, the bus driver, the port baggage handlers. And we had not even got to the ship yet.

The TV was following a Cuban who had hijacked a plane and wanted to come to Miami. He eventually gave up.

Time passed. Next morning I walked along the canal that separated the hotel from a golf course in the airport clear zone. I had first seen this almost 50 years ago. Landscaping was with primarily coconut and Christmas palms, Sea Grape, Ficus trees, and Crotons. Land crabs had dug burrows in the sandy canal bank.

We finally had to identify our bags for loading on the bus. The trip to the port was $10 each plus tip and took about twenty minutes.

Next came the embarkation check-in. ID the bags. Walk through a maze and up stairs and through the metal detectors and x-ray then more maze to the assignment of a room, dinner seating assignment (first seating was at 1745 at table 204), a notice that we would not get shore leave in Cartagena, and establish credit for use on the ship (They circumvented not tipping the ship personnel by a 15% surcharge).

We came on board and finally found our cabin. We were in 7148 on deck 7, port side forward with our own three foot wide balcony. It was now after 1300 so we went to lunch at the La Playa Grille on the Lido deck while they delivered our bags.

Boarding Area

We unpacked and moved in for the duration. There was adequate drawer and closet space, a compact bath with a shower, air conditioning and adequate lighting.

I crashed for a few minutes. It was suddenly 1730 and time to head for the Empire Diningroom on decks 2 and 3 aft. We were shown to our table and introduced to our two servers. We were not assigned tablemates for some reason and ate by ourselves the entire trip. The menu offered a selection of several hors d' oeuvres, soups, salads, entrees, deserts, drinks, wines and liquors. Overall the selection was varied, the food well prepared, the service was very good but not the quality I had expected.

Sailing time was 1700. It was delayed to top off the fuel. It was 1830 by the time we started down the channel. We finished supper watching coconut palms drift past.

We walked around the ship for an hour or so as the ship turned southeast at 22 knots. It was dark and the wake fluoresced a green with white trail a mile behind the ship.

That evening there were 8-10 foot seas. Overnight the NE wind freshened to 40-50 K. Carol put her seasick patch on. So much for Day 1.

Day 2.

The day began SW of Cayu Lobo with its huge Cuban flag whipping in the breeze. There was no sunrise with clouds and a 20-30k wind out of the north. We loafed along the northern coast of Cuba all day and moved into the Windward Passage (Passo de los Vientos) about 1800. We passed between Jamaica and Haiti during the night and into the Caribbean. New course was a little west of south straight to Cartegena. It was too deep to swim if I can't touch the bottom– 2500 fathoms.

The last time I was in the area was 1962 when I went to Guantanamo and chased Cuban mobile missile sites. On the way back to Norfolk we were in the recovery group for John Glenn's first orbital flight. The aircraft carrier I was on, the USS Forrestal, spent a couple days off the Outer Banks in March in 70k winds out of the NE gusting to 120k with 70-foot waves. That 1100-foot, 80,000-ton ship really rocked and rolled.

We checked the activities and Carol found a bridge group. I walked several miles around the weather deck and watched Cuba slide by. Wind across the deck was pretty fierce for walking. I was surprised they did not close the exposed deck 10. Walkers really got a workout with a 50k headwind. All the deck chairs were lashed down.

The wind had been 30-40k all day but stiffened in the evening with gusts to 82k that blew the tops off the waves. Seas were up to 15 feet.

The cruise was relatively smooth thanks to the stabilizer fins. Propulsion was by two 17.6 mw 360° electric Aziopods and three 1910 kw bow thrusters. This is powered by six 9-cylinder Wartsila diesel engines running the electrical power plant. Power transfer and maneuvering was smooth and quiet.

I requested an engineering tour to see the water, wastewater and solid waste and was told the EPA and Coast Guard did not allow this which is nonsense. It must be company of ship policy since the EPA has no prohibition. Later I asked for an interview with the engineering staff and was told this was not permissible. I did get a good tour of the galley looking at sanitation, solid waste handling, recycling, and hazardous materials. I will discuss this later.

We had lobster for the first formal meal of the cruise. The Captain was supposed to be there but I did not see him the whole trip.

Day 3.

It got light but the sun forgot to come out for a couple hours. There was high cirrus clouds with a NE wind at 45k. Clouds and sun angle change the sea color shades of light and dark blue or green depending on the depth. We went to breakfast about 0700 almost every morning on the Lido deck - cereal, eggs, etc. Twice during the cruise we went to the Empire dining room for the more formal breakfast.

About 0900 the wind dropped and some cumulus clouds were forming. I was surprised to see virga at sea with the rain evaporating before it hit the surface. Maybe the surface winds were blowing the rain away. Waves dropped to about 5 feet. Occasional small silver two-winged flying fish took off and skipped off the swells.

Pool and Fast Food

Here is a list of a typical days activities: A golf putting competition, ping pong and shuffleboard, arts and crafts, bridge, a hair seminar, trivia, dance class, chess and checkers, an art auction, sports trivia, an afternoon concert, cooking class, bingo, hairy chest contest, newlywed game, etc.

The library was mostly a collection of novels locked guests had left behind in cabinets over the computer terminals. You could not bother the computer people. No movies. No interest groups like poetry or natural science. Shows in the evening, including amateur nights, had mediocre entertainment at best. Could hardly stand the excitement.

The morning of Day 4 we arrived off of Columbia about 0700 and entered the channel near Isla de Terra Bolea. A White Egret flew across the bow. Several Common Terns, Black Skimmers and Laughing Gulls flew by. I noticed the channel markers were all solar powered.

We passed several mangrove-covered islands. Three men were pulling a beach seine on one. A Columbian Coast Guard helo flew over and a flight of Brown Pelicans crossed our stern.

We arrived in the outer harbor near the lighthouse and dropped anchor kicking up a lot of mud in the doing. We were at N10°23'00.3" W075°32'49.7" about a mile off the beach.

Cartagena

There was a petroleum smell in the harbor. A number of fishing boats maybe 20 feet long were pulled up on shore. A flock of Widgeons floated off the beach with Pelicans and an Anhinga sat on one of the fishing boats.

Another cruise ship was at a dock with several container ships. A passenger ferry crossed the mouth of the harbor. Behind the lighthouse was anchored a Columbian destroyer escort.

Stacks of three power plants and a big smoke cloud were to the south of downtown. The Fort San Felipe de Barajas built between 1657 and 1769 sat in the city center along with the Cathedrals of Plaza Bolivar. I was hoping to get to see the city but the docking was cancelled and we got a $25.00 rebate that probably covered the port fee.

The anchor was raised at 0940. We pivoted around using the bow thrusters and the Aziopods. We left passing a fort on one of the channel islands at the harbor entrance. The Island was home to a flock of Caribbean Grackles.

The pilot left at 1020. We began another afternoon and night of quality sea time on our way SW to Colón, Panama.

The weather warmed up and the sky was clear. Occasional flying fish launched themselves from the briny deep to escape some predator or maybe just for the fun of it. It was a nice afternoon with a showy sunset.

There was shipboard TV. One channel showed ship position. One had a forward view. One had a view aft. One was a CBS channel from New York City. Another was an ABC channel from Nashville. A movie channel showed the same three flicks 24 hours a day for the entire trip. Four channels showed official trip videos and periodically announced that these were on sale in the camera store.

Day 5

Another day where it just got light. We had passed the San Blas Islands in the dark. Lines of seaweed drifted past as we slowly approached the breakwater from the north into the entrance to Port Cristobal. The Ports of Manzanillo and Coco Solo and the city of Colón were out of sight to the east. We entered into Bahia Limón and sailed to the entrance to the first compartment of the three Gatun Locks.

There are several websites with good pictures like the following: http://www.plrphoto.com/Columbia,%20Panama%20Canal,%20 Costa%20Rica%20Pictures%20For%20Sale.htm, http://pages.prodigy. net/rmfz/cartagena.htm

Several White Egrets and Black Vultures were in the rocks and on the mud banks along the channel. Several Chapman's Swifts (<u>Chaetura chapmani</u>) flew around the ship as we waited for a big container ship to get through the adjacent lock. A cloud of smoke rose from burning sugar cane fields. I noticed the Canal Zone gate guard had a line of cars and trucks backed up. Several Black vultures cruised the sky and several were working the mud banks along the entrance channel. I noted a Tropical Kingbird sitting in the spiral of razor wire along the canal and a Costa Rican Tanager zipped past.

Most of the passengers were outside on the various decks watching the operation of the locks. The balconies sound nice but you can't see much to the front or rear and deck 5 had lifeboats obstructing the view.

Small boats picked up lines from our ship and attached them to diesel-powered locomotives known as mules. Each 55-ton mule could exert 70,000 pounds of force. Six mules are used to tow the ships through the locks.

Through the lock

The container ship pulled out of the first lock and the gates closed behind it. We were pulled into our lock and the gate closed behind us.

The adjacent lock drained into our compartment until they equalized. Valves were set and our compartment continued to fill until the gate opened into the next lock. The adjacent compartment emptied. The gate opened ready for another ship to enter. Each passage through the locks uses 52,000,000 gallons of fresh water all gravity fed to raise the ship 80 feet to Gatun Lake. We entered Gatun Lake at 0950.

Midway through the lock was the first of a series of range stations. Coded lights allowed ships using radio signals to determine their exact location. This system was being continuously upgraded.

One of the first structures visible from Gatun Lake was the dam on the Chigras River that controlled the lake level. There was a second dam on this river at Gamboa that controlled the flow into the lake from the 100 inches plus rainfall in the mountains.

The channel lead past Isla Tigre on the starboard (right) and the Isla Juan Galegas on the port (left). There islands and spoil banks and inundated forest are vegetated and habitat for birds and animals. We passed Isla Barro Colorado with the National Geographic research lab. Several small boats of young people paddled along the edge of the fairway. Gatun Lake ended and we followed the old Chigras River riverbed to Gamboa.

At Gamboa began the roughly ten-mile Gaillard or Culebra Cut across the Continental Divide to the Pedro Miguel Locks. The Cut required constant maintenance due to the unstable soil. It was recently widened from 152m (486 ft) to 192m (614 ft) to allow for two-way traffic.

<<>>

Map of the Canal

The Cut ended at the Pedro Miguel Locks. About 1430 the ship dropped into Miraflores Lake. Another mile or so was the Miraflores Locks into the Pacific. We entered the Pacific at 1600. The former Army Central Command Headquarters building on the south bank had been converted into a university. The old visitor center at the locks was being replaced. I was first there in 1969.

The channel widened and the Bridge of the Americas and the Ports Rodman and Balboa appeared in the distance.

It was evening and Frigatebirds and Laughing Gulls cruised the skies while several groups of Anhinga flew up stream. Several White Egrets looked like they were headed to a rookery. An Osprey sat on a power pole. About a hundred Brown Pelicans were floating or gliding in small groups.

We passed out into the Pacific Ocean passing the Amador Causeway to Naos Island. The lighthouse at the Port of Fort Amador disappeared in the evening haze. We were off to Coast Rica. No Panama shopping.

The canal

Bridge of the Americas

On April 6 (Day 6) we were off of Isla de Coba at N05°06'07" W82°26'13". Three Brown Boobies played in the air currents around the ship and even landing on the bow gear. Before long there were ten Boobies. When they went after fish they flew straight into the water. There were occasional small two-winged flying fish. Several large black dragonflies flew around near the water slide on deck 10 aft. (They were probably hitchhikers from Panama. I found several dead in the trash next day.)

Near the Costa Rican border off Punta Libre in the Gulfo Dulce we passed a large pod of dolphins. Maybe fifty animals were chasing flying fish that took off in all directions. Soon after we passed the dolphins we passed a large sea turtle. I asked the crew why they did not announce such sightings and was told they would be long passed before anyone looked. Maybe they think passengers are a necessary nuisance.

The April 7. Predawn sky turned pink then washed out to white. The sun did not appear for another two hours. Frigatebirds and Brown Pelicans cruised the skies announcing land nearby. Two white-rumped feral pigeons raced past the ship heading out to sea then turned back and beat us into port.

As we worked into the harbor and the dock there were more pigeons flying out over the water and Tropical Grackles flew along the beach. The port of Puntarenas (Sandy Point) was in the mouth of Golfo de Nicoya in Puntarena province and had been closed for about ten years. The dock was a concrete structure probably 2500 feet long and 30 feet wide extending from the beach. It was the only thing on Doña Beach until the Punta Caldera commercial port would be completed. The dock could accommodate two ships and was wide enough for two lanes of bus traffic.

We had breakfast early and were in the Pharos Palace to meet our tour at 0730. I was taking one called "Skywalk in the Forest". Carol signed up for the tour to Poas Volcano National Park with a lunch stop at Sarchi. We took water and cameras, our passports and the ship ID card.

Several websites describe this area of Costa Rica:,
http://tourism.co.cr, http://www.costaricamap.com, http://www.hotelpuntaleona.com.
This last has a checklist of 330 birds on the resort grounds.

Skywalk

My tour went from Puntarenas to along highway 17 to highway 23 along Playa Doña and the commercial port at the town of Caldera. There were several narrow railroad cars left from the time Costa Rica had a railroad.

Along the road were coconut trees, Tropical Almond, mango, citrus, papaya, tamarind, cashew, and banana. Flowering plants included yellow Esperanza, several colors of bougainvillea and hibiscus, red flamboyant and African tulip tree, and golden rain. There were several species of cactus, castor bean plants, kapok trees, huisache, and Honduran mahogany. Along the beach were coconut and almond trees and beach morning glory. A couple miles further we crossed the bridge over the Tárcoles River. We stopped to look at the colony of American Crocodiles in the river above the bridge. One of the crocs looked maybe 15 feet long. The guide mentioned pollution as a problem with crocodile distribution and survival. There was an effort to reintroduce them to some other rivers and a homing study to see if they are fixed on the hatching site and if they can find their way home after being moved.

Below the bridge a herd of Zebu cattle grazed and drank. Vegetated sandbars in the river supported white herons. Vaux Swifts flitted about and a kettle of Black Vultures was riding on a thermal.

Several vendors near the bridge had all manner of souvenirs from butterfly pictures to carved figures to T-shirts. The butterflies were caught wild instead of farmed although there were several butterfly farms in the area.

Along this section of road were cecropia trees, wild banana and papaya, and a pink tree called locally Indian crown. Mistletoe, bromeliads, and ferns grew on branches of some of the larger trees. We passed a field of melons, some good looking pasture and several herds of cattle.

A few minutes further we turned on to a dirt road for a couple miles to the Villa Lapis resort. We stopped for a stretch, water and pit stop then drove another mile to the Carara Biological Preserve.

This trip consisted of about an hour and a half easy hike through jungle crossing over 5 cable bridges over ravines. This same trip on the ground could take a couple days depending on the weather.

Our guide for about 30 hikers was a reformed stockbroker. He had a good general knowledge but was not a biologist. One problem was the group was strung out over maybe 50 meters of trail and since I brought up the rear I could not usually hear our leader. It was interesting but being near the end of the dry season and at mid day there was no bird or animal activity. I was fairly familiar with the vegetation and conducted my own tour with about a dozen tail draggers. I saw some new plants such as Vanilla orchids and philodendrons in their native habitat, Balsa trees, and Elephant ear trees whose seedpods were shaped like a large brown ear.

We returned to the Villa Lapis for a vegetarian lunch and rehydration. There was tea and lemonade, two kinds of pineapple, two kinds of bananas, and papaya and mango slices. I tried one of their local beers – terrible.

While we were eating near the stream a couple iguanas were spotted in the trees. A gray basilisk or Jesus Christ Lizard (<u>Basiliscus</u> sp.) with a big neck ruffle and that walks on water went crashing through the vegetation and across the stream surface.

After about 45 minutes we headed back to the ship. Costa Rica history and culture was discussed and the cost of real estate and living on the economy.

Three rivers empty into the bay and a large fresh water marsh near the port. There were White Egrets, Blue Heron, and a Rosette Spoonbill in the marsh edges and Vaux Swifts filled the air.

We were delivered back to the ship. I dropped off my binoculars and cameras and got a bite to eat then walked back to the beach. I walked about half a mile on the beach in both directions and found no shells. The beach was muddy dredged sand with little drift marking the high tide lines. Leaving the beach to enter the stalls along the malecón I found a sand dollar and a half of a Reticulated Venus (<u>Periglypta</u> <u>edmondsoni</u>).

Carol's trip to the Poas Volcano National Park with a lunch stop at Sarchi was programmed for eight hours. After riding for a couple hours the area was in fog and the caldron was not visible. There was a stop at the village of Sarchi where oxcarts and other items were carved and painted. There was a delay and her bus was the last to return to the ship.

Dinner in the Empire room was frog legs or prime rib. We sailed for Acapulco about sundown.

On 8 Apr. (Day 8) the morning chose not to have a sunrise again. We were heading Northwest about 20k into a 20 k wind from the NE. We had passed Nicaragua and were off the Gulfo de Fonseca where Honduras and El Salvador come together. I saw some Pacific Shearwaters feeding and some green flashes in the dark swells, possibly tuna probably feeding on the same baitfish.

The sky was overcast and cool. We were out past the continental shelf but mountain peaks of El Salvador and Guatemala occasionally showed to the starboard. Two more sea turtles drifted by. A dark cloudbank sat on the northern horizon like a Blue Norther was coming. During the night the wind picked up to 35-40k with 10-12 foot waves.

On the morning of 9 April winds were up to 65k and the weather decks were closed. We were in the Gulf of Tehuantepec back over the continental shelf off the coast of Oaxaca, Mexico. Around noon we the wind hit 82k blowing the top off 15 foot waves. About 1600 we were heading west off of Puerto Ángel out of the Gulf of Tehuantepec about 200 miles south of Acapulco.

About 0600 on 10 April we entered Acapulco Bay. No wind. Clear skies. Pelicans and Frigatebirds wheeling around. Buildings clawing up the hills in all directions. The dock was across the street from the old fort that had been changed to a maritime academy and museum.

Acapulco Bay

We signed up for a city tour that included the cliff divers and a side trip to Coyuca lagoon, a beach and resort maybe ten miles to the north. We met in the Pharos lounge and followed our leader off the ship and through the Mexican customs and visitor center.

Everyone loaded up thirty to a bus and went to see the cliff divers. Cliff diving began about 50 years ago when some young fishermen were trying to impress the girls. There is a relatively sheer cliff about 130 feet above the water into a narrow (20 foot) channel 12 feet deep with a sea cave at the end.

Look at the Website:

http://community.webshots.com/album/1854551ZvJhESBAyk

The divers (las Clavidistas) wait until the waves are just right then they have to get out about 20 feet to miss the wall. My first impression was that this sure is dumb but like hot doggers anywhere they make money doing something different and they mostly do it safely. There is a shrine to the Virgin of Guadalupe at the top and divers go off several ledges as singles or groups depending on skill and seniority. An entrance fee is charged to maintain the diver's retirement and medical insurance.

The individual divers expect tips and sell autographed photographs. Only the senior diver draws a salary.

Divers

We loaded up and drove north along the Pie de la Cuesta, a sandy beach about 20 miles long out to the tip of a peninsula with the 28 square mile fresh water Coyuca Lagoon inside. Along the road was a Mexican Air Force Base. This was the set used for several Rambo and similar movies.

Also along this road was a new squatter village on a barren section of public land. These are called parachutitas because the people seem to fall from the sky and develop a homestead. If they survive living on their homestead for five years it's theirs. Some of the homesteads were pretty fancy for squatters.

A mile further north was a resort that went for $300 a night. Strange neighbors.

On the way back to town we stopped at a place for a coke and pit stop. It was on the lagoon side with rental boats and jet skis. I walked across the road through another restaurant to the beach. Nice tan sand along the Pie de la Cuesta. There was a steep forebeach with pounding surf. Nothing on the beach but the palapas. No flotsam. No shells. I looked along the seawall and found a limpet and half a Donax shell indicating a sandy bottom with big rocks.

On the ride back there was discussion about the economy, real estate and construction cost, wages, etc. Our guide pointed out the homes or former homes of some of the movie stars.

Our next stop was the city market with several jewelry stores. I got the impression they should be paying us to take the tour.

We were back at the ship in time for lunch. We still had the afternoon and half the night left until we pulled the anchor. We went back ashore and took a taxi to the old market. We looked at several shops and noticed that the Mexican souvenirs changed every year. We hit a shop with jewelry and found some opals with good prices. Since we can resist most everything but temptation we bought some. I also found several antiques from Colima and Jalisco supposedly about 500 years old.

Dinner included Alaskan deer (Caribou) steak.

Every evening when we got back the beds were turned down with chocolates and a towel animal of some kind like dogs, swans, crabs. One afternoon there was a class showing how to make 16 different animals. This, like the napkin folding, was interesting but of marginal utility and promptly forgotten.

On 11 April we were supposed to sail about 0400. A number of passengers had wanted to spend the night ashore so we left at 0700 for run to Puerto Vallarta. A little after 0800 we passed a small pod of dolphin. About 1100 we were off San Francisco Bay and a flock of 30-40 brown boobies began to work around the ship and stayed until sunset.

It was 0700 on 12 April when we began working our way into the port area at Puerto Vallarta commonly called PV. Frigatebirds and pelicans were out in Bandaras Bay. Pacific Grackles and Laughing Gulls met us on the shore.

I signed up for the expert walking tour up into the foothills of the Sierra Madres Mountains. The scenery was good but none of the trail was above a class three. There were areas with loose pebbles. No one mentioned we might have to ford the Mascota River several times. The river rocks were smooth but I found I was tender footed barefooted.

We rode out six miles to the village of La Desembocada with the bikers and horseback riders. There was a bullring and an airport on the way. Our hiking party consisted of two guides, a Japanese couple and I. We were driven about a mile to the end of the road and began an uphill climb for about 30 minutes to the high point on the trail, about 2000 feet.

On the way up I saw a Tufted Flycatcher and Beechey's Jay. Some of the vegetation was familiar but I found some new ones - the ear tree, a viney Bougainvillea, organ pipe cactus probably a species of Pachycereus or Lemaireocereus, large bracket fungi, termite nests located in the tree tops to escape the ants, and a new species of mistletoe. There were Pacific madrone, gumbo-limbo or sunburned Indian trees, mahogany and some prickly pear cactus.

Both guides spoke fair English and had an interest in the environment. I asked the leader if he had had college. He said one year then he got married. The other was still working on a degree.

There were several overlooks where the valley showed between the trees. We could see much of the Mascota River including the horseback group.

As we worked our way down to the valley floor we stopped at a hot spring that had been improved and converted into a spa. Banana trees and bougainvillea surrounded the spring. Rancho Sierra Madre had a grove of citrus trees and a number of banana and papaya trees. One large ear tree had a nest of the Altamira Oriole. A flock of Pacific Parakeets flew in by twos twittering. A Pileated Flycatcher flew through.

We walked along the river until we came to a ford. This old tenderfoot need a little assistance to ford the stream bare footed but I did not look forward to sloshing along in wet shoes. About a mile along a road beside the stream we met a pickup, two guys on horseback, and a couple dozen head of cattle. The cattle made a run for the water then they and two cowboys walked up stream.

A Guatemala Ivorybill Woodpecker flew across the road into the woods. Several Mexican Caciques chased a Black-throated Magpie-Jay across the river. Several whiptail lizards darted along the road. A fence lizard sat blending into a tree trunk.

We reached a second ford. Downstream in a shallow area with willows stood several White Ibis and Great Egrets. Just about the time I got my shoes off for another ford the truck came along, drove across the river and picked us up for the ride back to the starting place.

Back at the cantina I ordered two tacos and a Carta Blanca beer. I thought the Carta Blanca brewery had closed down years ago. Maybe just in Monterrey.

We were back to the ship just in time to catch my wife and take a "Gallery tour". No one said anything about most of the galleries and museums being closed for siesta on Saturday afternoon.

We stopped at the north end of the Malecón and walked north and east to a small unimpressive gallery on Hidalgo then to the Galleria Indigena on Hidalgo and Corona with all of this year's chic pottery, then west on Corona to a gallery on Morelas with a lot of good modern art, then to a restaurant overlooking the Malecón and the bay. We got a quick (Mexican quick) coke and I dashed over to the Huicotyl Indian shop and museum then back to the bus. We all decided to stop on the island in the Cuale River that is several blocks of shops and the closed natural history museum.

PV Beach

Lovers Arch is in the hillside north of the island. There was the bridge between the houses of Liz Taylor and Richard Burton during the shooting of *Night of the Iguana.*

After twenty minutes there we rounded up most of the group and headed to another gallery that was closed. It just happened to be across the street from a high-end jewelry store. The store had some excellent amber. Then we stopped at Plaza Genovesa near the dock. This has a lot of shops and two big jewelry stores. We were back on board the ship in time for supper. This was another excursion they should have paid us to take.

We looked at the Sheraton Bougainvillea where we stayed several years before. The wing we were in was severely damaged. A hurricane in November 02 had roared in from the west with a high tide and 30-foot waves and had destroyed most of downtown and beachfront property including a public school.

I watched the undocking from the upper deck. The trees at the Maritime Terminal were filled with Pacific Grackles that sound different from our Texas grackles. A large concrete block where the bow lines were tied appeared to be the roost for several species of birds. They had settled in and were disturbed by the line handlers. A Socorro Storm Petrel, several Red-Footed Boobies and Pacific Shearwaters, a bunch of Brown Pelicans and some Black-legged Kittiwakes. The birds left as three men came out to cast off the bow line. The line was taken in as the men went to cast off the breast line. This line was taken in and between two tugs and the bow thrusters we moved away from the dock into the night. Some of the pelicans and Shearwaters returned to their roost.

About 0700 on Sunday, 13 April, we were approaching Mazatlan in Sinaloa state about 200 miles north of PV. We passed the lighthouse and old Mazatlan on the starboard. On the port we passed Isla de los Chivos, Isla de los Venados, and Isla de los Pajaros. We were in the channel passing Isla de la Piedra and finally docking at the cruise ship docks. An interactive map of Mazatlan is at http://www.maps-of-mexico.com/. We docked at N23°11'49.4" W165°24'38.7".

A pair of pigeons flew out past the ship, turned around, and beat us to shore. Frigatebirds floated on thermals over the water and several Shearwaters played around the ship.

Furniture factory/shop

We booked a tour up Highway 40 (the Highway of Death) to the foothills of the Sierra Madres. First stop was an adobe brickyard. They produced both sun-dried adobe and kiln-fired bricks. They both begin the same with a mixture of clay, sand and organic such as rice hulls, hay, and manure. It is mixed by hand until just right then turned into molds set on a sanded surface to prevent sticking. The forms are removed and the bricks are dried over night. They are then moved and allowed to dry for another week. The bricks can then be used or stacked to form a kiln and baked. The clay quarries provide clay and hold water for making the bricks. When a clay quarry is worked out it is used as s rice paddie. A worker can produce 1000 bricks a day earning about $10. These workers are part time alternating with farming work.

There are a number of adobe brickworks and several sand and gravel works in the riverbed and several cement block plants to provide the material to keep Mazatlan growing.

We passed through groves of citrus and mangoes and truck gardens of tomatoes and peppers. These are harvested and shipped fresh by truck all over Mexico and the US.

Our next stop was a furniture factory and pottery. A machine shop cut the rough furniture pieces that were then hand finished. Some of the chisels looked handmade. They used local mahogany, ear tree and raintree (amapa) wood. They sold the furniture by the truckload and also sold pottery made on site. A potter was demonstrating making pottery by the slab technique. Further down the road were several other similar shops.

I finally identified a dooryard tree that was bare with small green fruit. This was the local plum called ceredo.

We drove several more miles out into the foothills. The highway was narrow two-lane with no shoulders most of the way, no guardrails with a 35mph speed limit and lots of truck traffic. There are 20-30 fatalities and numerous accidents every year. There were about 150 crosses marking death sites. This was the only road connecting north central Mexico to the coast. They were beginning a new toll road near Mazatlan but it will probably take years.

We passed through the Village of Concordia strung along the road and spread over the hills. The school used satellite TV and teacher aids instead of full-time teachers and was apparently successful. We passed a church and other buildings mostly painted in bright colors.

A little further on the van turned off the highway to the old mining town of Copala. It began as a Spanish gold mining town in 1565. It was taken over by an American mining consortium but was literally destroyed by Pancho Villa as part of his cultural reform. Favorable weather and picturesque cobblestone streets with old buildings have attracted Americans to settle here. There was a central square and church, a restaurant and hotel, several gift shops and the normal bakery, general store, etc. We had lunch of what I considered rather bland Mexican food with no tortillas until I asked for them. The salsa was mild and the chips were tough. I had another Carta Blanca beer.

Along the route I saw vultures, a Black-throat Magpie-Jay, a Tufted Flycatcher, and a Northern Mockingbird. The principle cactus was an organpipe cactus locally called cardone probably a species of either Pachycereus or Lemaireocereus. There were a few large prickly pears in tree form possibly <u>Opuntia</u> <u>megacantha</u>.

We stopped for a 25-minute shopping opportunity at Mazatlan's Golden Zone. I skipped the jewelry stores in favor of seashell world. Shelling laws had changed and prices had really increased in the past few years. They had no large shells and no coral. Tourists were nooot allowed to take shells from the beach.

Back at the ship we had supper and I came up to deck ten to watch the ship leave port. Several Vaux Swifts played around the ship. A Sinaloa

Crow flew over supervising the operation. Several Black-legged Kittiwakes and pelicans were working the harbor.

The 14th of April was another quality sea day. It's only about a hundred miles to Cabo San Lucas so we turned north up the Sea of Cortez or Gulf of California for about a hundred miles to near Isla San José then circled back almost to Mazatlan before heading directly west. They may have been hoping to see whales but it was a little late in the season. About 0800 I saw an American Egret headed north but several miles off shore. There are no islands in the area and no freshwater for many miles. Later in the day two Frigatebirds were cruising to the west. About 1600 we passed a large sea turtle.

I stopped at the pizza bar for lunch and asked for jalapeno and anchovies and was told they only had cheese or pepperoni or a calzone.

This was formal night but again I did not see the captain. I guess the captains of smaller ships eat with the passengers.

On the 15th of April we dropped anchor in the harbor of Cabo San Lucas N22°53'03.3" W109°59'58.8". The trip to shore was by lighter or water taxi that carried about 40 people a trip. Frigatebirds rode the thermals. Laughing Gulls and pelicans accompanied the fishing boats and lounged on the dock.

Our tour was the coastal highlight tour. Our guide pointed out the major hotels and eateries including a bagel shop. The first 20-minute stop was at one of two glassblowers in town. It was interesting to watch them work and surprising how little time it took to make a piece. They had a large variety of products for sale. House Sparrows and pigeons were at home in the courtyard.

The next stop after passing a couple golf courses was at a condo resort on Playa Médano with a nice vista of the harbor and Barco Verado. We drove another 15 miles past more golf courses and resort complexes and a botanical display with Elephant trees and organ pipe cactus and an herbal shrub called Damiana (Turnera aphrodisiaca) that is a cure-all tonic like Ginseng. There were a couple iguana lizards on one of the big cactus. There was also a Gila Woodpecker.

We passed more resorts along Bahia Santa Maria and Bahia Chiléna and Punta Palmillas on to San Jose del Cabo and the Playa Costa Azul on Bahia San Jose del Cabo. We passed another golf course in town on the way to the mission and town square. Another 20 minutes to shop and back to Cabo San Lucas for more shopping. You can find interesting maps like the interactive http://www.cabobob.com/00BajaHwy/mapframes.htm, and http://www.loscabosguide.com/maps/maps.htm.

Meanwhile back at the ship another liner had dropped anchor and another was holding offshore. We took the lighter back in time for lunch while they pulled the hook in mid afternoon. Another 40 hours at sea and we would be in San Diego.

I saw a dark cloud on the north horizon that looked like an old Blue Norther. A couple hours later the wind came up and we spent **16 April** rocking and rolling.

We packed up and had the bags ready for pickup by midnight. We arrived on **17 April** about 0700 to sunny skies that disappeared by 1000 with showers. After breakfast we checked the room once more, got our carry on bags, got in line for customs and began waiting for our color section to debark. We were next to last to go about 1100.

The last steps were to go into the terminal, find our bags and head for home.

Comments

I was aggravated about not getting to see engineering or at least talk to some of the engineering staff and the ship blaming this on the EPA.

I was disappointed that we did not get ashore in Cartegena as advertised. We were not advised of the change until we were on board. A $25 per person rebate does not make up for the loss. This was probably the port tax refund and not compensation for our lost port call.

Anyone taking a cruise should be aware of the total cost. The advertised price was $1399 each. Then there were $279 port charges each and a tax of $279 each plus cruise insurance of $128 each totaling $2085 each or $4170 per couple plus expenses.

Then there is transportation to and from home to the ports. San Antonio to Miami was $356 each and San Diego to San Antonio was $146 each totaling about $1004 but I had enough frequent flyer miles to cover the tickets.

An extra day on each end contingency time had a cost for hotel, local transportation and meals of $150 each day or another $300.

There was a $10 charge each in Miami for the bus to the port. Add a %15 tip for the crew, the tours and miscellaneous expenses like $1.50 for a coke plus tip, etc that totaled about $1800.

This totaled about at almost $3600 per person for a $1399 cruise special. The planning cost appears to be the suggested cruise price multiplied by 2.6.

I forgot to mention a travel glitch. The package was purchased from American Express who listed it as a 16-night cruise leaving on 1 April. Carnival listed it as a 17-day cruise. This led to confusion in scheduling the airline reservation and resulted in a ten-minute call from the ship at $7.00 a minute to the airline to change the flight time. The change could have resulted in a fee of $35 each for changing reservations but did not. Since the next available flight was on the 18th we had to spend a night in San Diego.

The term 17-day cruise itself was misleading. We spent most of day 1 getting on the ship and situated and not sailing until sundown. Day 17 ended at sunup and took until noon to get off. The 16-night terminology is more accurate.

I reached the conclusion that I am not a cruise person. Cruise activities were mostly gambling, drinking, eating, art auctions, and a hairy leg contest in the pool. The ship did not announce weather, flocks of birds, sea mammals, or other things of interest to me. I don't mind sea time if the goal is worth it but not days at sea for a few hours shore time. Having been temporarily assigned to two aircraft carriers and a destroyer escort I have had plenty of "quality sea time." If it had not been for bird watching and reading the trip could have been a real drag.

Bird list

Procellaridae
Pacific Shearwater   Puffinus pacificus
Hydrobatidae
Socorro Storm-Petrel   Oceanodroma socorrensis
Pelecanidae
Brown Pelican   Pelicanus occidentalis
Sulidae
Brown Booby   Sula leucogaster
Red-Footed Booby   Sula sula
Anhingidae
American Anhinga   Anhinga anhinga
Fregatidae
Magnificant Frigatebird   Fregata magnificens
Ardeidae
Great Blue Heron   Ardea herodias
Great White Heron   Ardea occidentalis
Snowy Egret   Egretta thula
Anatidae
American Widgeon   Mareca americana
Pandionidae
Osprey   Pandion haliaetus
Cathartidae
Black Vulture   Coragyps atratus
Laridae
Laughing Gull   Larus atricilla
Common Tern   Sterna hirundo
Black-Legged Kittiwake   Rissa tridactyla
Rynchopidae
Black Skimmer   Rynchops nigra
Columbidae
Domestic Pigeon   Columba livia
Psittacidae
Pacific Parakeet   Aratinga strenua
Apodidae
Chapman's Swift   Chaetura chapmani

Vaux Swift	Chaetura vauxi

Picidae

Gila Woodpecker	Centurus uropygialis
Guatamalan Ivorybill	Campephilus guatamalensis

Tyranninae

Tropical Kingbird	Tyrannus melancholicus
Tufted Flycatcher	Mitrephanes phaeocercus

Mimidae

Northern Mockingbird	Mimus polyglottos

Plooceidae

House Sparrow	Passer domesticus

Icteridae

Pacific Grackle	Cassidix graysoni
Mexican Cacique	Cassiculus melanicterus

Thraupidae

Costa Rican Tanager	Tachyphonus axillaris

Corvidae

Beecheys Jay	Cissilopha beecheii.
Black-throated Magpie-jay	Calocitta colliei

The trip was interesting but I have had enough quality sea time for now.

BIGFOOTING AROUND

Three Hundred Miles

a Day in

Western Washington

Carl Lahser

Dedicated to

the Memory of

Dr. Donald D. McLain

the best teacher I ever had.

This "trip report "contains a prose and poetry remembrance of a ten day trip to Tacoma, WA, and coastal Washington state, 31 May to 9 June 1995.

Poems

Scars upon the Earth
Rain in three parts
Scotch Broom
Iron Bridges
Mount St Helens
Mount St Helens Bulls
A "Cool "Mountain
Rain Forest Green
Roosevelt Elk
Sea Lion Pup
La Push
The Makah Radar Site
Neah Point
Banana Slug
Spring Highway Flowers
Tacoma Quartet
Mount Rainier Spring Suite
    1. Wet Snow
    2. Canyon Snow
    3. The Mountains
    4. An Early June Afternoon
Center Pivot Irrigation Working

Bigfooting

Around

Three Hundred Miles a Day:
Western Washington

I was scheduled to attend an environmental conference in Tacoma, Washington, from 5 - 9 June, 1995. With a lot of vacation time saved up I decided to take advantage of the transportation opportunity and see some of the western part of Washington. I left on Wednesday, May 31st, for the Seattle -Tacoma airport.

The plane left about noon on a track east of San Antonio and Austin to the Dallas-Ft Worth International Airport (DFW). We crossed over a lot gravel pits and other construction scars that were plainly visible on the wet earth. Some unengineerlike thoughts follow.

SCARS UPON THE EARTH

The gentle summer earth is green
and a thousand shades of tan
unnaturally cut into a patchwork quilt
by ecotones
and thoroughfares
and tillage patterns.

Serene but for the scars
of the quarries and the borrow pits
their unnatural shapes glaring in the sun
insulting the surrounding symmetry
and those pock marks of oil drilling stands
and subdivision cul-de-sacs
Like scars of honor that mar the cheek
are the obvious marks of planetary violence
as roads and highways,

canals, dikes and dams,
and power line right-of-ways
draw attention to intentional desecration
in the name of progress

+++++

The approach into DFW was over flooded fields and under an overcast sky with rain falling in the distance. We landed on wet runways with rain cells in the distance.

Rain in Three Parts

I
From gray, amorphous clouds
falls rain looking like a horses tail
flipping slowly in the wind.
Sometimes the rain
blows away or evaporates
before it hits the ground

2
Look ahead.
In the distance the horizon
becomes blurred then
disappears into a cloud
as rain cells drop their loads
heavy rain within the lighter showers

3
After the rain
standing water reflects,
reflects sunlight
like a broken string of mirrored beads
ponds and cattle trails red
beneath reflected silver
liquid silver strands in furrows of a new field
Water to make the summer green

+++++

Two hours were gained heading west. We arrived about 1800. It was still light in Seattle and it would stay light until about 2200. Sunset was 2059. (It would begin getting light about 0430 with sunrise at 0515.)

My rental car was a Nissan Sentra that flew quietly down Interstate Highway 5 (I-5) for the twenty miles to Tacoma. Many of the road cuts along the Interstate were covered with dry grass. Temperature had been in the 80's for a couple weeks with no rain. The radio had just reported that the fire danger was high, the first large forest fire of the season had burned about a thousand acres and a fire fighter in Manitoba had been trapped and killed.

After a night in Tacoma I was up early and stopped by McChord AFB for some shopping. Heading south the traffic flew along about 65 mph but there were no speed limit signs posted. Several informational signs indicated what gas stations and restaurants were available at each exit.

Along the roadsides and up into the trees grew a bright yellow flowering plant up to five feet tall. I had never seen it before. The plant was Scotch Broom, <u>Cytisus</u> <u>scoparius</u> (L.) Link [<u>Genista</u> <u>scoparia</u> (L.) Lam.]. A naturalized European legume it came in several varieties or forms. It had been imported and planted widely to stabilize road cuts and clearcut forest sites. This it does well but it out competes the native vegetation. It had been planted widely as an ornamental and is very impressive in early summer. Scotch broom was recently classified as a noxious week and an eradication program started. State road crews were spraying it with herbicide as part of an eradication program but local nurserys were still selling it. Herbicide loaded trucks cruised the roads spraying Scotch Broom, Salmon berry and other roadside vegetation.

SCOTCH BROOM

Along the highways
Up the hillsides
Bright yellow splashes in the forest edge
Scotch Broom,
Cytisus scoparia
bright yellow six foot sprays
planted for soil erosion control
and as an ornamental
now called a noxious weed
Ambivalence

+++++

California poppy was planted along the road for color with a variety of grasses for erosion control. A vetch and Foxglove (<u>Digitalis</u> <u>purpurea</u>) were also common.

Down about Centralia a volunteer litter crew was cleaning the roadside with a yellow litter bag about every hundred feet along a couple miles of highway. Every little town had some individual or group adopting two mile stretches of highway.

There were two huge balloons floating about 200 feet up off of the Interstate. They both marked trailer or RV sales locations.

Several state parks and community colleges were noted with highway signs. A number of large northern-style red barns appeared on farms but many appeared somewhat rundown. The houses looked modern and freshly plowed fields were evident as were large pasture plots.

I was distracted by two turn-of-the-century iron bridges, one highway and one railroad over the Toutle River.

Iron Bridges

Topping a hill I see
two iron bridges
protruding from the trees

a highway bridge painted silver
and a rusty railroad bridge
both spanning the Toutle River

Bridges from my childhood
far away in time and space
spanned another river
flowing through another wood
in another place.

+++++

The bridges made such an impression that I missed the signs for Seaquest State Park, Toutle and the Mt St. Helens National Volcanic Monument. The next exit was ten miles down the road at Kelso. I stopped at the Chamber of Commerce visitor center and looked at their display. The lady attendant provided directions and a number of maps and brochures on the park and the Olympic Peninsula. I backtracked ten miles to the proper turnoff.

Crows in ones and twos were fairly common as were solitary robins. A green heron and several swallows flew across the road indicating nearby wetlands just before cattails and a marsh came into view.

I turned off at Exit 49 to state road 504. The road is called the Spirit Lake Memorial Highway. The Mount St. Helens Motel was right on the corner with a gas station.

Five miles along was a visitor center with a post card view of Mount St Helens and a marsh on the Toutle River. The marsh supported Red-winged Blackbirds and a blue heron in the cattails Several swallows were skimming the water surface.

Inside the visitors center were interpretive displays and other information about the eruption on 18 May, 1980. An earthquake on 20 March was followed by steam vents and ash eruptions and more minor quakes. At 8:32 A.M. on 18 May there was a 5.1 earthquake that triggered an avalanche. It removed 1300 feet (9677 ft to 8364 ft.) from the mountain top and left a 1.2 by 2.4 mile crater 2000 feet deep. A half cubic mile of debris was deposited into and flowed down the Toutle River eventually blocking the Columbia River.

A volcanic blast followed immediately which put a quarter of a cubic mile of ash into the air. The blast front reached a speed of 250 mph and with a temperature of up to 680 degrees F. It wasted 235 square miles of forest. Fifty-seven people were directly killed. Spirit Lake rose 200 feet from debris and generated a wall of water 200 feet high. The Toutle River was filled with as much as 600 feet of debris and mud that roared down 14 miles of river bed and averaged 150 feet of mud. Steam and ash plumes rose at speeds up to 600 mph to an altitude of 15 miles.

MOUNT ST. HELENS

In the distance is the mountain
that blew its top in 1980
and leveled the forest for 15 miles around.

The ash and lava has disappeared
under new growth
but white skeletons
of the dead forest
still lie in state

+++++

A mile further along the road two mule deer sauntered across the road. Another mile further was the town of Toutle with visitor information, souvenir shops and a few houses. There was also a school and fire department. It's 25 more miles to the Coldwater Ridge visitor center. A wall of water and mud raised the river 23.5 feet at Toutle within seven hours of the quake.

First sight of the Toutle River showed gray rocks and a swift, cold, milky water. The milky appearance came from fine silt or "rock flour" suspended in the cold river water.

At mile 19 was a shop called the Mile 19 House. A sign read, "Last chance for gas or towing service".

A couple miles further was a turnoff to a photo opportunity. This was an overlook for a large stilling basin and dam designed to remove ash from the Toutle River. The dam had been constructed when up to 600 feet of ash and debris stopped the river. Engineers were afraid that this plug would kick out and release a wall of water and mud. An overflow structure was provided to allow cleansed surface water to be discharged down stream.

Along the trail to the overlook several trees were identified by signs. Oregon Oxalis, Draba, Chickweed and wild strawberries were abundant in the cool shade. Crows and robins were the only birds to be heard.

The Hoffstadt Bluffs rest area and overlook was 15 miles from the visitor center and located at the end of the actual landslide. Concessionaires offered helicopter rides and a "tent and breakfast" service.

Several prefab concrete bridges were newly installed along with a new blacktop road. All the bridges had been destroyed by the avalanche except the Hoffstadt Canyon Bridge. It was damaged and replaced by seven concrete sections totaling 370 feet long. This bridge marked the end of the blast damage. The blast leveled 150 square miles of timber.

A Western Giant Swallowtail Butterfly (<u>Papilio</u> <u>cresphontes</u>) crossed the road near the turnoff to the new North Fork Ridge Forest Learning Center. The Center had just been open for two weeks. It was a model of partnering being jointly sponsored by the Weyerhaeuser Corporation, the Washington Department of Transportation, the Rocky Mountain Elk Foundation and the National Park Service the Center. Informative displays showed forestry processes, efforts to salvage blowdown timber and steps taken to stabilize and revegetate the damaged to the area. Thousands of pounds of grass and clover seed were air dropped and millions of tree seedlings were planted. Coupled with the natural forces of the plant and animal survivors the land turned green and animals have returned. Looking down into the river valley a herd of over a hundred bull elk could be seen lying in the gray ash.

Across the valley thousands of downed trees lay parallel like a hardwood floor among the new growth and newly planted trees. The downed trees became nurse trees that gradually decayed and enriched the soil to support new vegetation. Life was never completely gone since many plants and animals spend the winter underground.

Mount St. Helens Bulls

The old herd died in the blast
but a new herd has taken its place.

A hundred bull elk lay
in the sun in the warm gray ash
along the Toutle River
waiting patiently for green grass
and the fall rutting season.

+++++

The insect population appeared to be recovering. Damselflies were common and several beetles and bugs were seen along with the butterflies.

The next stop was at the Elk Rock Viewpoint. Piles of landslide debris and more downed trees were still evident 15 years after the eruption. The gas cloud was over 500 degrees F and traveling over 200 mph as it passed this point.

After crossing Elk and Marrata Creeks the final stop was the new Coldwater Lake Visitor Center that had opened the previous week. The mountain was still about six miles away. The center looks at the mountain across Coldwater Lake. Coldwater Creek was spared from immediate damage from the avalanche by being in the shadow behind Johnson Ridge but was dammed by the landslide. A lake that formed behind the dam was almost 600 feet deep.

The thirty mile trip back to the Interstate was uneventful. I left I-5 again at the Kelso exit. Kelso and Longview were small towns with more fast food franchises than many larger cities. The Port of Longview had what I thought were several grain elevators. They turned out to be for handling wood pulp. This was an important port for loading timber and pulp wood.

I crossed the Columbia River to Oregon on the Lewis and Clark Memorial Bridge, an old, two-lane iron bridge, and took Oregon 30. It was about 50 miles to Astoria.

A strange truck configuration flew past. It had small wheels on the back of the tractor and two sets of tandem wheels in the trailer.

The little town of Clatskanie on the Clatskanie River was notable for $1.49 gas. A few miles further was Westport with a ferry across to Cathlamet, WA. The forest and hills along the south side of the road rose almost straight up. There was a mix of conifers and hardwoods. On the north side of the road was the flood plain of the Columbia River.

The port town of Wauna was busy loading various transport ships. Just west of town was the top of Clatsop Crest at 650 ft. Clatsop State Park was located on the river. Next came Swenson and a range of hills that flowed into Astoria.

Astoria, OR, was where Captain Robert Gray discovered and claimed the Columbia River for the US in 1792. It was also the wintering place for the Lewis and Clark Corps of Discovery in 1805-1806. John Jacob Astor established a fur trading post there in 1811. The area was settled in the 1840's and the first post office west of the Mississippi was founded in 1847. The maritime museum and a light ship were closed by the time I arrived as were the Astoria Column on Coxcomb Hill and Fort Clatsop National Monument.

The road back to Washington crossed the Columbia on the Astoria-Megler Bridge. A couple turnoff areas provided good views of the bridge and the river mouth with its shipping traffic. Ft Columbia State Park was the site of Ft Columbia built in 1904. It functioned through both world wars and never fired a shot. Ft Canby was near Ilwaco and built in 1875. These two forts, plus Ft Stevens across the river near Astoria, were built to protect the Columbia River access. There were also the Lewis and Clark interpretive center, two light houses and Washington's first salmon hatchery.

Driving to Long Beach and Ilwaco I looked for the beach. I found that there was limited access and that most of the beach could not be seen from the road. Some of the beach was closed to protect clam growth when there was access. I was going to go out to historic Oysterville but it was getting late and the "beach" road was more like a tunnel though the trees.

I stopped to look at the North Head Light. This historic structure was sold several years ago and was privately restored and maintained. The light had been removed to a museum. Built in 1898 it was only 65 feet tall but was located on a bluff that raised the light to 194 feet. Its light was visible for twenty miles. The trail to the light house was about a quarter mile through the woods. Ranunculus, Geranium, Oregon Oxalis and bush blueberries grew in the damp shade. A wet wind was blowing about a half gale and with temperature in the 50's.

I turned back to Seaview and got on US 101 towards Aberdeen. The road passed through the Wilapa National Wildlife Refuge for several miles along coastal marshes then crossed the Naselle River to Nemah. For another 20 miles the road ran through the woods along Wilapa Bay where chanterelle and other mushrooms were commercially harvested. The road crossed several branches of the Nemah River. The village of South Bend was missed in a blink. Raymond, a small town on the Wilapa River appeared prosperous.

A few more gray overcast miles took me to Montesano on state highway 8 back to Tacoma. At 350 miles the car was low on gas so I filled up at Montesano for $1.29 a gallon (gas was $1.06 in San Antonio) and got back on the main road. There was light traffic to Olympia. Many fields were covered with golden stands Scotch Broom. A large power plant air cooling tower showed over hills to the south. Traffic picked up on at Olympia on Interstate 5 to Tacoma.

I was up early Friday morning and got ready to leave. Looking out to check the weather I saw a "Kool" cigarette billboard along I-5 under the peak of Mt Rainier.

A "Cool" Mountain

As I look out through my hotel window
I see Mt Rainier, majestic white
against a cobalt sky.
Directly below this splendid scene
was a billboard advertising
"Kool" cigarretes

+++++

Friday morning traffic to Aberdeen and Hoquiam was light. A swampy field near Montesano was covered with yellow iris.

Aberdeen was a disappointment. The tall ship signs lead nowhere and there were no tall ships. The sign for a museum again lead nowhere. I finally found the visitors center and they confirmed the tall ships were out and the museum would not open for another two weeks. A number of unique houses dated to the turn of the century. Aberdeen had a population of about 15,000 and was located on the Chehalis River. Its major industry was wood products.

Four miles down the road was Hoquiam, population about 7000. I passed on through and turned on to Washington 109 for the coast. The road stopped on the beach road at Ocean City Beach Park. The beach was flat with tan and gray sand and flat black cobbles. The tide varied from +7 to -0.5 feet. It was going out so I looked for anything on the beach. There was nothing of interest so I turned south to Oyhut and Ocean Shores.

The beach was half a mile away through the trees on either side of the road. Ocean Shores idea of a town was a mile of tourist businesses along the highway leading to a wildlife refuge on Browns Point and the passenger ferry operates in the summer. The ferry ran across the mouth of Grays Harbor inlet to Westport and Twin Harbors State Park on the tip of Point Chehalis.

A flea market was located at the intersection with WA 109. Eight temporary structures of 2X4's and plastic sheet housed vendors that sold sunglasses, T-shirts, wood carvings, smoked meat, etc.

At Copalis, five miles north on highway 109, I stopped and asked where the scenic vistas were. The visitor center lady said that Copalis Rocks were just a few miles north and had world famous vistas. The three access roads were now posted private property.

I considered driving on up to Moclips and Taholah on the Quinault Reservation but the people in a small restaurant said there was nothing outstanding to see and the road from Moclips through the Quinault reservation was not very good. The recommended route across to US 101 went via Copalis Crossing and along the Humptulips River to the town of Humptulips.

Copalis Crossing consisted of an abandoned garage, a general store and several houses. Humptulips was not much bigger but some nice houses were visible from the road.

The road towards Neilton passed through replanted clearcut forest. Cutting stopped at the border of the Olympic National Forest. I turned off at the road to Quinault, the Quinault Rain Forest and the Colonel Bob Wilderness.

A couple miles beyond the village of Quinault was a visitor center with several short interpretive nature trails. I took a half mile trail that recommended a 30 minute walk. I was still using a cane and took almost an hour.

Rain Forest Green

Trees.
Tall trees blanketed
in dull green clubmosses.
Trees 500 years old
200 feet tall
ten feet in diameter.

Dark green of mature conifers.
Light green of new growth.
Fluorescent green of
Bigtooth Maples back-lighted
by a shaft of sun light.

Brown green of slugs on the forest paths
Yellowgreen of the new fern fiddleheads
Living green, Live green

+++++

The trail lead through big trees covered with clubmosses and licorice ferns, along a stream channel and into a forest of River Ferns.

Three criteria define a rain forest: having over 100 inches of rainfall; the presence of nurse trees; and high humidity for clubmosses and other epiphytes that cover the trees. Nurse trees are decaying fallen trees that act like sponges to hold water for dry periods. Young trees grow and flourish in the remains of remains of the nurse trees. A few cut stumps maybe ten feet tall and eight feet in diameter had young trees growing out of the top of the stumps with roots running down the sides. Olive green slugs were crawling along the bark mulch paths. The only birds to be heard were robins near breaks in the forest. A small gray wren flitted across the path into the brush. This forest was much lighter than the spruce forest. The trees grew to near 200 feet.

I stopped at the park headquarters at Falls Creek for lunch and was told that there was a wash out on the north shore road around Lake Quinault. With that news I went back the way I had come to 101 and up to the Queets Rain Forest on the Queets River.

The Queets Corridor road was a dusty dirt road. It roughly followed the Queets River about thirty miles to a primitive camp ground. The drive was interesting but dusty.

While returning on this dusty road to civilization three young bull elk stepped out of the woods in succession, crossed the road and disappeared into the shadows. The last elk paused in a stunning broadside silhouette before making his exit. Any hunter would have been thrilled.

Roosevelt Elk

Along the road near the Queets River
an elk stepped into the road,
crossed and quickly disappeared into the forest.
Another followed and, likewise,
quickly disappeared.
A third elk stopped in full profile
and looked directly at me
then regally stepped behind
the curtain of trees.

The play continues.

+++++

It was seven miles to the town of Queets and another five to Kalaloch. The visitor center at Kalaloch had the best and only display of sea shells I found in the area. The former school teacher attendant at the center recommended stopping at Ruby Beach about 15 miles further along.

I parked at the Ruby Beach access. A short walk through the woods lead to a descending path to the beach. The path stopped at a jumble of large logs at the high water mark. Logs, some maybe four feet in diameter, had escaped down rivers to be driven high on the beach by storm tides. This wooden barrier helped protect the beach and the headland from erosion and provided unique habitats for pioneer species of plants and animals.

The beach beyond the logs was tan and gray sand with biscuit sized flat gray stones. Seastacks, large pieces and spires of rock that were once part of the shore, provided a unique scenic character to the beach. The tide was retreating with minimal wave action or roar of the waves. The sky had turned gray with a stiff breeze.

It was after five and I still had fifty miles to go to La Push. The road passed through an alternation of clear cut and second growth timber stands. After pausing for some road work and seeing a state truck spraying roadside vegetation the road passed an airport south of Forks. It was surrounded with Scotch Broom on the clear zone perimeter. Two biplanes were parked near the road.

A forest products museum and visitor center were located across from the airport on the south edge of town. Several blocks of stores and several restaurants made up this regional shopping center. I crossed the Sol Duc River and stopped on the north side of Forks for supper.

Tribal highway 110 lead six miles to the community of Mora with a snack bar and general store. There were three access roads to the ocean in the ten more miles to La Push. I arrived about seven and checked into Shoreline Resort, a Quileute tribal enterprise.

A drive through town covered the few blocks of paved streets, past the tribal center and the fishing fleet to a dead end on the Sol Duc River.

A trail from the resort passed through beach blueberries and beached trees to the beach. In the falling dusk a young female sea lion pup lay on the beach watched carefully by the tribe's biologist and police.

Sea Lion Pup

On the dark rocky beach at La Push
lay a four month old sea lion pup.
Forty pounds of dirty white fur
with black spots and large dreamy eyes
she helplessly watched the beach
waiting for night, the tide,
and Momma
to return.

+++++

Maybe thirty fishing boats were nestled behind a breakwater reinforcing the mouth of the river. The crab traps were a different style than I had seen before.

The beach was much like Ruby Beach with gray and tan sand and flat basalt biscuits. I walked a mile south towards Teahwhit Head then back to the breakwater.

The resort was two two-story buildings that had been devided into eight apartments each. Mine had a bedroom and bath with a kitchen/dining room in about 250 square feet with electric heat but no TV or telephone. I was up at 0530 and on the beach by six. There would be no sunrise with the clouds but it was light enough to see that the sea lion pup was gone. Temperature was about 55°F.

After walking the beach for an hour I took a path through the bushes behind the logs. Waist-high blueberry bushes formed a hundred foot wide break above the normal high tide. The path was sandy and numerous strawberry plants, <u>Fragaria</u> <u>vesca</u>, were spreading their green tentacles. The berries were ripe and delicious.

La Push faded in the mirror a little after eight. I was heading for the Hoh Rain Forest. In Forks I bought gas and had breakfast. It was seven miles south to the Hoh turnoff and thirty more east to the park visitors center. The drive through the woods passed some really big trees. A sign said one spruce was 220 feet tall, 12.5 feet in diameter and 400 years old.

La Push

To sleep to the shush of waves
cold from the far Pacific;
to wake to the cry of the gull;
to crash through the huckleberry bushes
on the way to the beach
and find ripe wild strawberries;
to walk gray sand beaches
covered with flat gray stones;
is to touch the Quileute world
little changed in a thousand years.

+++++

The visitors center had several long and short trails. I took a short one called the Hall of Ferns. It was a quarter mile and took about twenty minutes. That felt good so I took another trail with a couple from Minneapolis that was about three-quarters of a mile long. Beautiful weather and just the right temperature for a walk in the woods.

Back on 101 I stopped at the Timber Museum and visitors center just south of Forks. Displays showed local history, the development of the timber industry in the Northwest and the process of logging.

At Sappho state highway 113 took me to the town of Clallam Bay on the Strait of Juan de Fuca. The road into town lead down to the waters edge. Everything for the tourist but a place to eat. The charter boats were doing a brisk business and most of the motels had "No Vacancy" signs.

Back on the highway I stopped at a beach and took a walk. I found several shells, beach worn but still shells. A leafed basalt formation was tilted and exposed to the weather. A list of shells is at the end of this missal.

Retirement homes lined the seaward side of the highway right up to the border of the Makah Reservation. Many of them were expensive homes overlooking the Strait. Most were "high bank" lots but a few had access to the water.

A number of seastacks sprouted from the water, a result of seismic action and erosion. Many of these rouge rock formations had vegetation growing on their top.

The Makah Reservation was doing much better than when I had last visited it in 1977. The radar operation and five acres around the radome had been transferred to the FAA. All the remaining land had been given back to the tribe. The former Makah Air Force Station became the Thunderbird Resort.

At the entrance to the town of Neah Bay was the new Makah Cultural and Research Center. The museum housed much of the collection retrieved from a Makah village covered by a mudslide 800 years ago. Clothing, wooden tools, baskets and other delicate artifacts indicated this was a relatively advanced culture with many surprises for the investigators. This was a very nice facility and had cost $2.5 million but another million was needed to complete some of the exhibits.

The Makah tribe was not closely related to other tribes on the Peninsula. Trade goods had been identified as coming north from

California and southwest from western Canada. Apparently they were an advanced trading people and traveled widely.

Next came lunch on the Neah Bay waterfront. I watched charter boat activity while eating an oyster poorboy. Lots of traffic.

I drove around town and out to the old radar site/resort. The homes and buildings looked about the same but the general store had burned an been replaced with a mini-mall.

The Makah Radar Site

The radar site is unchanged in twenty years
except the Makah tribe now runs the base
as the Thunderbird Resort.
Time travel to the 1960's with no TV or phone
Tourists sleep in the barracks
and the FAA runs the radar.

+++++

Stopping at the Thunderbird Resort the buildings looked like we left them twenty years before. It looked like a nostalgic retreat to the 1960's. The manager said they did a good business, both weekend and weekly rentals.

A dirt road continued past the resort entrance and out to the Tatoosh Island overlook. A trail went about two hundred yards then branched with no indication of which way to go. Both branches were well traveled and I took the wrong one for a few minutes until I met some people coming back. They said it was rough going and did not lead to the overlook.

Back at the intersection someone had blocked off this wrong trail. A half mile walk through the woods and over a bog lead to an overlook. The trail felt spongy like walking on a pile of wet saw dust with several feet of rotted wood under foot. It sometimes had a hollow sound. Several boardwalks and bridges across boggy ground needed a major overhaul.

Neah Point

On the trail to the end of CONUS,
filtered through firs and
shoulder -high bush huckleberries,
the barking of seals can be heard.
No seals can be seen
but a large sea otter
is lying in the sun grooming itself
out of the crushing swells.

+++++

Near the trail end I could hear seals barking. I looked for them from the point but could see only one sea otter sunning itself.

The overlook was a point of rock about 100 feet above the water. The water was a deep blue with floating clumps of kelp. The eternal waves had gouged out caves under the point of Cape Flattery and there were large slabs of stone lying in the water.

There was a good view of Tatoosh Island from this overlook. Tatoosh Island marks the southern side of the entrance to the strait and is the most north and west point in CONUS. A Coast Guard Station and light house sit on the island but most of the Coast Guardsmen live in Neah Bay and commute by helicopter.

Several banana slugs shared the paths and a deer mouse ignored me as it sat nibbling on something. The slugs were about 3-4 inches long and yellow with black mottling.

Banana Slugs

Down the trail through the rain forest
a banana slug is blocking the trail.
Yellow with large black spots,
an imposing three inch presence.

+++++

I stopped by the Thunderbird Resort to report the trail condition. They did not seem surprised or likely to fix the problem any time soon. I began the 70 mile drive to Port Angeles. The sun was setting but it would not get dark until about nine. I met about twenty cars and was only passed by a pair of motorcycles during the 70 mile trip. The two lane highway was almost a continuous curve with numerous hills covered with woods, clear cut areas and a few farms.

When I had driven this road twenty years before much of the land was in mature tree. There were trucks hauling timber and the growl of logging machinery that sounded like Bigfoot's mating call in the still of the afternoon. In another twenty years the trees may be back.

It was after nine when I arrived at Port Angeles and checked in. There was a restaurant next to the motel but it and everything else was closed for the evening. I checked out early Sunday morning to go to Hurricane ridge and on to Tacoma.

The five miles from the motel to the Olympic National Park entrance was mostly through residential areas of Port Angeles. The next thirteen miles to Hurricane Ridge wound through woods. The roadside was with covered with wild flowers. The road lead through two short tunnels and hosted a number of scenic views from the numerous turnouts. Snow fields, streams and waterfalls appeared in the steep valleys as the altitude increased. The Dungeness village and the Dungeness National Wildlife Refuge were clearly visible twenty miles to the northeast.

From the visitor center literally a hundred snow cover peaks were visible. The road beyond the center was covered with snow as were the three trails near the center. Walking tours along these trails would not start until late June. Canada and the Straits of Juan de Fuca were hidden under a layer of clouds.

A herd of deer were generally ignoring the human visitors as they grazed on the exposed vegetation. One doe appeared ready to drop a fawn.

Several flowers were peeking through the snow: the Glacier Lily, Erythronium grandiflorum, and the Lance-leafed Springbeauty, Claytonia lanceolata. The temperature was in the mid thirties with a twenty knot wind. Dandelion or, more likely, the mountain or false dandelion, Agoseris sp., was blooming in the parking area.

A little lower on the mountain and out of the snow Martindale's Lomatium, Lomatium martindalei, and Western Wallflower, Erysimum capitatum, grew in the roadside gravel. Spreading Phlox, <u>Phlox</u> <u>diffusa</u>, and Smooth Douglasia, <u>Douglasia laevigata</u>, were growing out of cracks in the rock face along the road. An Indian Paintbrush, <u>Castilleja</u> <u>hispida,</u> and Lyall's Lupine, <u>Lupinus</u> <u>lyallii,</u> were blooming in fill material. At a turnout were bushes of Salal or Wintergreen, <u>Gautheria</u> <u>shallon</u>, in bloom. A bumble bee was feeding on its flowers.

Further down the mountain were a number of drooping white heads of Oregon Fawnlily, <u>Erythronium</u> <u>oregonum</u>, in the shade of some conifers. Beargrass or Turkey-beard, <u>Xerophyllum</u> <u>tenax,</u> and Ox-Eye-Daisy, <u>Leucanthemum</u> <u>vulgare</u>, grew roadside as they had near Queets.

In standing water and mud of a seep along the road were Elkslip Marshmarigold, <u>Caltha</u> <u>leptosepala</u>, Western Monkeyflower, <u>Mimulus</u> <u>guttatus,</u> wild strawberry, <u>Fragaria</u> <u>glauca</u> and the Pioneer Violet, <u>Viola</u> <u>glabella</u>.

A little lower were Wooly Sunflowers, <u>Eriophyllum</u> <u>lanatum</u>, Dutch Clover, <u>Vicia</u> <u>sp</u>, Salmonberry, <u>Rubus</u> <u>spectabilis</u>, and a wild plum. Cow Parsnip, <u>Heracleum</u> <u>lanatrum</u>, was just budding at altitude but in full bloom nearer sea level. Sedum grew out of the rock faces. Western Serviceberry, <u>Amelanchier</u> <u>alnifolia</u>, bloomed in the shade. Several belly plants grew out of cracks in the walks (Seline?).

Spring Highway Flowers

Flying down I-5 with the rest of the pack
I noticed one thing the Interstate doesn't lack
WILDFLOWERS!
Scotch Broom and Golden Poppies
break up the green.

Along US 101
I had lots of fun looking at
WILDFLOWERS.
Foxglove and Beargrass,
Thimbleberry and Huckleberries
Ox-Eye Daisy are often seen.
Park roads have wondrous color
white, red, pink, yellow and lavender

WILDFLOWERS.
Blooms vary by day and altitude
a kaleidoscopic technicolor time machine.

+++++

Near the park entrance were ferns and horsetails and Bigtooth Maple replaced the subalpine firs. Common Yarrow, <u>Achillea millefolium</u>, that had been occasional at 3000 feet was common in the flatlands. Palmate Butterbur, <u>Petasites frigidus</u>, was through blooming. Another strawberry, <u>Fragaria vestus</u> (?), was in fruit.

Driving back through suburban Port Angeles to US 101 I passed a sign for the Port Angeles Museum of Art. I located the museum after several blocks detour and found that it would not open for another hour. Sequim and Dungeness were just a few minutes down the road so I did not wait.

Sequim is in the rain shadow of the Olympia Mountains and gets about 18 inches a year. They have an annual Irrigation Festival. Most of the farming was dry land farming with some cattle. I stopped at the Sequim Museum and Art Center. They had a permanent historical exhibit and a current student exhibit plus an archeology exhibit of a local mastodon dig. The old couple running the museum were interesting to talk to. The book store had a very good collection of local Indian lore, archeology and natural history.

Dungeness was about five miles north and the home of the Three Crabs Restaurant. Their clam and crab boil was outstanding. I talked to the people at the next table from North Dakota. He had been through boot camp at Lackland and had worked for a chemical company in Corpus Christi. A list of shells is on page 42.

It began to rain as I left the restaurant. Mist or rain continued all the way to Tacoma. US 101 lead through Blyn to Discovery Bay. I got on WA 104 to Shine and Port Gamble then onto WA 3 to Bremerton and WA 16 to Tacoma.

The conference began Monday morning with a field trip to the Jim Creek radio facility in the Cascades two hours north of Tacoma. I had been there the previous November so I did not go

Tacoma Quartet

1
Where is Mt Rainier today?
Yesterday it lived in a clear blue sky
flying over fair Tacoma and
Puget Sound cold and deep.

2
Old red and yellow brick buildings
with arched windows and
fancy cornices and column caps
next door to sleek modern concrete and glass

3
Union Station.
Renovation.
Now a Federal courthouse
of red brick and a copper dome.

4
Coffee shops with no poetry
have no soul.
How impersonal can you get?

+++++

I spent most of the overcast morning walking around looking at the old buildings of down town Tacoma with Scott Sheppard, the Randolph AFB historic preservation officer. We noted the clash in historic periods and architectural styles.

The weather began to clear after lunch and we were off to Mt Rainier. Directions from the hotel that took us twice the mileage to get to the park entrance. We went down I-5 almost to Olympia to WA 510 to Yelm then WA 702 to WA 7 into the park.

Lunch stop was at Elbe in the Railroad Diner. A series of railroad cars from the logging days were lined up along the road. They served what was probably the greasiest hamburger and fries I had ever eaten. Grease literally dripped out of the bun.

The road paralleled the Nisqually River and we entered the park through the Nisqually entrance. The ranger said it had hailed in the past hour but the sun was out at that moment. The first mile into the park was sunny but along the road pea-sized hail was blown into the shady spots under the trees and even blanketed the road in a few places.

The trees were white near the mountain tops. Clouds of snow were floating along blocking out the heights.

From one overlook you could see the Nisqually River valley with an artistic wash of snow flakes. The river and a bridge looking miles below us. Large, wet snowflakes were drifting in the air threatening to hide the valley.

Mount Rainier Spring Suite

1. Wet Snow

Wet snow was piled inches out
on the north side of Douglas fir trees
pointing into the storm

Snow piled high on the top of boughs
bending them to the ground
telling of the forest calm

+++++

The town of Longmire was lost in the snow as we drove past. So was the Cougar Rock ranger station.

We stopped at the turnout for Narada Falls but did not take the snow covered trail to see the falls. It was cold and the snow was blowing. Snow flakes flew upwards outlining the wind currents blowing out of the Paradise River canyon. The snow rose about ten feet above the rim then curled outward piling the heavy wet snow on the inside of the rock retaining wall.

Mount Rainier Spring Suite

2. Canyon Snow

Snow flies upwards
out of the Paradise River Gorge
and up Narada Falls
curling over a protective wall
and plastering snow
on the wall's rock and mosses

+++++

A couple slow miles further was Paradise and the Henry Jackson Memorial Visitors Center. Jackson's wife had called this place paradise but she must have seen it under better conditions. Large fluffy flakes drifted slowly on a light breeze at 27 degrees F. We parked and went in to look at the displays and the movie on the mountain. Paradise was about a mile high and averaged 620 inches of snow each year. The power was off and sales in the gift shop were kept in a notebook. Must have done this before. Displays showed what we would have seen when the visibility was more than 200 yards.

This could have been the end of the road but we decided to continue down the mountain to the south east corner of the park and then north along the east side of the park on WA 123 and 410 to Tacoma.

Snow was left behind as we cruised past Reflection Lake and Lake Louise. They still had ice along their shorelines. A series of switchbacks lead down and out of the trees to the Valley of the Ohanapecosh River. At the Grove of the Patriots we saw old-growth Douglas fir, western red cedar and hemlock trees as much as a thousand years old.

Mount Rainier Spring Suite

3. The Mountains

Clouds, rain and snow are integral
to the rhythm of the mountains,
to the relentless flow of time,
to the music in your mind.

+++++

Visibility was low under low clouds and mist but the road was clear to the Stevens Canyon cutoff. The road was closed shortly after we came through.

Rain and fog began as we headed north and was with us all the way to Tacoma. We climbed up to the tunnel on Cayuse Pass in snow and rain mixed. The roads to Sunrise and White River were not yet open for the season. Two Elk crossed the road barely visible in the dusk and mist.

Lumber trucks rode our bumper on the descents sometimes flying past in the mist. We usually caught them on the next hill.

Mount Rainier Spring Suite

4. An Early June Afternoon

Weather rides heavily on late spring clouds
Sunshine precedes pea-sized hail.
Sleet slides down the slopes
and covers the road.
Large fluffy floating flakes of snow
hide Paradise.
Rain washes the eastern slopes.
Fog hides two roaming elk.
Night comes slowly in the mist.

+++++

The first town out of the park was Greenwater on the White River. I was going to stop for gas but there was not station. It was another rainy twenty miles to Enumclaw then to Auburn and I-5 to Tacoma.

Fourteen hundred miles in western Washington in five days had flown by. The next three days of the Legacy environmental meeting were eventful and successful. I flew back to San Antonio on Friday morning.

The air route back was different than I had been on before. We went straight south from SEATAC between snow covered Mt Rainier and Mt St. Helens and crossed the Columbia River at the Hood River with a dam and the Snake River visible far to the east. Near Redmond, Oregon, we turned to the southeast across the Nevada flat lands and south of The Great Salt Lake to Grand Junction, CO. The path continued to Montrose, CO, and down the fertile San Juan Valley to just west of Alamosa. Sand Dunes National Monument and Pikes Peak were clearly visible. A course change to eastward lead to Taos, Amarillo, Wichita Falls and DFW airport.

Center Pivot Irrigation Working

Four dark green circles inside section lines
with light green wedges of water spray
trailing down wind
wetting the thirsty prairie
Hundreds of circular fields
to make the desert bloom
suck the aquifers dry
spending our children's legacy

We crossed several areas of intensive agriculture using center pivot irrigation. A couple of the systems were disbursing water.

It was a beautiful day for sight seeing, frosting on the cake for a naturalist working vacation. Oil field grids of roads with bare squares of the pumping stations, contour plowed farms, center pivot farms, ranches with well worn trails to isolated stock tanks, and other man made features with their distinctive characteristics. The mountains, deserts, rivers and cloud formations decorated the frosting.

Its always nice to get a little fun in your work and this trip was a winner.

carl
950610

Shells of the La Push and Sekiu Beaches

Phylum Arthropoda

Balanidae
Tetraclita squamosa rubescens Darwin. Thatched barnacle. Dead at Sekiu beach.

Chthamalidae
Chthamalus fissus Darwin. Common on rocks and mussels at La Push and Sekiu.

Phylum Mollusca

Buccinidae
Volutopsius stefanssoni (castaneus) Morch. Chestnut Melon Snail. One live near Sekiu. One dead at La Push.

Fasicolaridae
Fasicolaria sp. Dead at La Push.

Olividae
Olivella pedroana Conrad. Purple olive. Dead near Sekiu.

Tellinidae
Macoma brota Dall. Frail Macoma. Dead at La Push and Sekiu.

Veneridae
Paphia staminea petiti (Deschaynes). Rock Cockle. Dead at Sekiu.
Prothaca staminea Conrad. Pacific Littleneck. Dead at La Push.

Myacidae
Mya truncata Linne (Panomya artica ?) Arctic Rough Mya. Dead near Sekiu.

Solenidae
Siliqua patula Dixon. Pacific Razor Clam. Three partial at Sekiu.

Modiolidae
Modiolus modiolus L. Horse Mussel. La Push and Sekiu.

Acamaeidae
Acmaea scutum patina (Eschscholtz). Plate Limpet. Live near Sekiu.

Dungeness Shells

Ostreidae
<u>Ostrea lurida</u> Carpenter. Puget Sound Oyster. Dungeness.
Pectinidae
<u>Pectin rubidus</u> Hinds. Pink scallop. Puget Sound near Dungeness.